VICTORIAN SHOPPING

Maurice Baren was born in Harrogate, Yorkshire. After a long career in horticulture and landscape management, he has now dedicated himself to discovering many aspects of our social history and bringing them to the notice of an increasing number of readers. His earlier titles are *How it All Began*, his first book about the history behind certain brand names, *How it All Began in the Garden*, the stories behind plant names and the people who collected plants or grew them in their nurseries and gardens, *How it All Began Up the High Street*, the stories behind the shop fronts, and, in 1997, *How Household Names Began*, the stories behind products found in every home and *How It All Began in Yorkshire*, which tells the stories behind his home county's businesses.

Author's Note

It is always a challenge to write such a book as this. As an author you want to bring together previously unpublished facts about the subject, but you also realise how much has been written on the area in the past; any such book must be a blend of both.
I am grateful to those who have allowed me to use their research and their writings, especially to the late Alison Adburgham who was most supportive and generous in allowing me to use her material, to Bill Mitchell, and also to David Kennedy for the loan of *Vanity Fair* magazines.
To friends who are ever watchful eyes, passing on useful snippets of information, I would particularly thank Dr Fred Kidd, John Hopkinson and Tom and Peggy Hewitt.
I am grateful to the companies whose stories are retold in the book for information and for the loan of illustrations.
As always I have been grateful for the encouragement and help of the staff at Michael O'Mara Books – this book was Michael's own idea, and I hope I have done it justice.
My wife Judith has helped me in so many ways with this book, especially with the endless searching through old journals for information and illustrations. Her help has saved many hours and enabled the book to be completed within the timescale – many, many thanks.
I have tried to ensure that proper acknowledgement has been given, but if anyone feels I have failed to give them credit I do apologise, and hope that it will be possible to amend in future editions.

Bibliography

Benjamin Shaw's Almanack, 1892
C. & J. Clark, 1825–1975, Brendan Lehane
Chambers' Journal – contemporary issues
Dalesman, December 1995
Festival of Britain Guide to the Pleasure Gardens of Battersea Park
Fine Silks & Oak Counters – Debenhams 1778–1978, Maurice Corina, Hutchinson Benham Limited, 1978
The Food Makers. A History of General Foods Ltd
From Eden Vale to the Plains of York, Edmund Bogg
The Girl's Own Paper, February 1897
The Graphic – contemporary issues
Hatchards, 1797–1997, Anniversary brochure
The History of Bovril Advertising
A History of Heal's, Susanna Goodden, 1984
A Hundred Wonderful Years, C.S. Peel, The Bodley Head Ltd, 1926
A Hundred Years in Princes Street, 1838–1938
The Illustrated London News – contemporary issues
The Infants' Magazine, 1888
The Land of Long Ago, L.L. Weedon
Liberty's – A Biography of a Shop, Alison Adburgham, Unwin Hyman Limited, 1975
My Store of Memories, Rowan Bentall, W.H. Allen, 1988
Pears: The first 200 years
Punch – contemporary issues
The Sandboys, H. Mayhew and G. Cruikshank, David Bogue, *c*1850s
Scarborough – Ancient and Modern, Jas Chapman
Seventy Years Agrowing or An Early History of Timpsons, W.H.F. Timpson, 1952
Shopping in Style, Alison Adburgham, Thames & Hudson, 1979
Shops and Shopping, Alison Adburgham, *1800–1914*, George Allen & Unwin, 1964
Spons' Household Manual: A Treasury of Domestic Receipts, E. & F.N. Spon, 1891
A Story of British Achievement 1849–1949, Harrods, 1949
The Story of Sunlight Soap
The Strand Magazine – contemporary issues
Henry Tate 1819–1899, Tom Jones, Tate & Lyle Limited, 1952
Tiny's Tales in One Syllable
Vanity Fair, 1869
The Yorkshireman, 2 August 1893

VICTORIAN SHOPPING

Maurice Baren

Michael O'Mara Books Limited

First published in Great Britain in 1998 by
Michael O'Mara Books Limited
9 Lion Yard, Tremadoc Road
London SW4 7NQ

Illustrations copyright © 1998 by BEAMISH, The North of England Open Air Museum, County Durham:
pp. 138, 139 (*below*); Chris Beetles Ltd, London/Bridgeman Art Library, London/New York: p. 103;
Bird's: pp. 21, 23, 30; The Boots Company Archive: pp. 81 (*below*), 86 (*right*); Bridgeman Art Library,
London/New York: front cover – top left, pp. 15 (*below*), 34, 50, 82 (*below*), 110, 114, 115 (*below*), 119 (*below*),
130, 135 (*below*); Cadbury Ltd: back cover – below left, p. 27; The Co-operative Union: p. 140;
Mary Evans Picture Library: pp. 11 (*below*), 38, 55 (*right*); The Fotomas Index: pp. 117 (*both*), 121 (*below*);
James & John Graham Ltd: p. 35 (*top*); Harris Museum & Art Gallery, Preston: pp. 126, 127; Harrods Limited,
Company Archives: front cover – below, p. 116; Johannesburg Art Gallery, South Africa/Bridgeman Art Library,
London/New York: p. 111; Kraft Jacobs Suchard Ltd: p. 27; John Lewis Partnership Archives: pp. 113 (*both*), 118,
119 (*top*), 120 (*both*), 121 (*top*); Popperfoto: pp. 20, 41 (*below*), 77 (*below right*), 97 (*below right*); Tate and
Lyle Sugars, Thames Refinery: p. 39; Topham Picturepoint: pp. 109, 133 (*top*); The Vintage Magazine Co.: front
cover – top right, back cover – below right, pp. 35 (*below*), 74 (*below*), 131 (*top*), 134.

A CIP catalogue record for this book is available from the British Library

ISBN 1-85479-302-0

1 3 5 7 9 10 8 6 4 2

Designed and typeset by Martin Bristow

Printed and bound in Italy by L.E.G.O., Vicenza

Contents

Introduction

The reign of Queen Victoria lasted over sixty years. During that period (1837–1901) many changes took place in the technological development, prosperity and social structure of Britain; some village shops of that period became well-known names in the twentieth century, either as major shopping groups or as popular product brands, such as Debenhams and Cow & Gate.

In an age when everyone shops, it is easy to forget that in the early part of Victoria's reign many rich and middle-class people went to the larger stores, but did not go in; they expected the proprietor to bring to their carriage door goods from which they could select their purchases. Other suppliers were commissioned to design and make furniture and would bring samples to those who lived in the big houses or estates; provision merchants, the butcher, fish-monger and others were expected to bring their goods to the servants' entrance at the rear of the house where they would be dealt with by the housekeeper or cook. Magazines and newspapers of the period generally contained a wide range of advertisements, showing that many purchases must have been made by post; these ranged from patent medicines and cure-alls to bicycles, furniture, clothing and household goods.

In contrast, the poor at that time had little or no money to spend. Those who worked in mills or early factories were often under an obligation to their employers to buy from them or to have groceries or other domestic items as 'payment in kind' for work done. The mill owner's 'shop' often represented terrible value for the work that had been done. Even lower down the scale the very poor lived from hand to mouth and would only rarely be able to shop. They could not afford new clothes and their diet was very basic, often consisting of bread and potatoes, with little or no meat.

During the reign of Queen Victoria a sense of adventure prevailed and many new items were brought to the country from distant lands. The Great Exhibition of 1851 furthered this interest

In the 1870s, the gas companies were still assuring the public that they could supply 'an illuminant quite equal to the electric light, and much more agreeable, at far less cost'. Indeed the City Commissioners of Sewers decided at one stage to discontinue the use of electric light on the Holborn Viaduct as it was 7½ times more expensive than gas! Only when street lighting and better surfaced roads were provided did shopping become the social experience we know today.

It wasn't until the end of the nineteenth century that electric lighting was common in shops. With electricity came the opportunity for 'modern devices', such as lifts and escalators – the *Glasgow Herald* in 1855 described Wylie &

and led to new furnishings, materials and foods being sold in Britain's stores and shops as the concept of 'going shopping' caught on. It also led to the acceptance of the new 'warehouses', a synonym for a shop in this era, and the vast ranges of stock, often displayed in magnificent showrooms. The enormous galleries at the Crystal Palace – neither made of crystal nor a palace, but an immense hall of iron and glass with ten miles of display frontages – set new standards of display, with visitors being able to browse without obligation to buy.

Shop windows in the early years of the reign were generally made up of small panels of glass, normally 30 cm (12 inches) wide by 40 cm (16 inches) deep. It was only in the 1830s that plate glass was introduced and gradually shops changed to having, initially, three panes of glass, before having, at the end of the reign, larger single sheets which encased the whole frontage of a shop.

A WALK DOWN REGENT STREET.

roads and the introduction of the railways which enabled manufacturers, and smaller traders, to expand their trading area; they also enabled people to visit the larger towns and cities to do their shopping, and return home within a few hours. It was only at the end of the century that the motor car made its appearance. Initially considered 'a new fangled and most unreliable contraption', in later reigns it would transform our shopping habits.

Lochhead's early 'lift' installation, in their premises in Buchanan Street, as 'a very ingenious hoisting apparatus . . . not only intended to lift bales . . . but to elevate those ladies and gentlemen to the galleries to whom the climbing of successive flights of stairs might be attended with fatigue and annoyance. Parties who are old, fat, feeble, short-winded, or simply lazy, or who desire a bit of fun, have only to place themselves on an enclosed platform or flooring when they are elevated by a gentle and pleasing process.' Harrods in London installed the first 'moving staircase', in 1898, the forerunner of the escalator.

In the mid years of the last century, transport was revolutionized by the improvement of

Social concerns existed throughout the period. In 1879 there was the hardship caused by economic decline in Glasgow and industrial centres in the north of England; this showed itself by shops in London having large sales of household goods at very reduced prices, items people in the north could no longer afford. During this period there was great poverty and pauperism in many areas, and emergency feeding projects had to be carried out. However, there was also concern at the level of drunkenness. To counteract this, coffee taverns were opened, for example in Clare Market, off London's Drury Lane, for 'supplying refreshments of various

In contrast, toy dealers, perfumers, jewellers and silversmiths served the minority higher income classes, and the number of these in any one town was very small.

Some shops, such as the ironmonger and the tailor, were where the items on sale were also manufactured, often specifically for individual customers. For instance, some shoe shops would have 'lasts' for regular customers, designed to ensure the boot or shoe was a near perfect fit.

Many shop workers lived in dormitories over the shops – some even slept under the counters – and the working conditions of the assistants were hard with long hours and low wages. However, some people saw new opportunities and some of today's shops, such as Liberty's, W H Smith, Burberry and Harrods, are examples of Victorian enterprise.

This book brings together tales and facts about life in Victorian shops gathered from many varied sources. The story is illustrated with contemporary advertisements and other material to enable us to see what life was like between 150 and 100 years ago. It was very different from what we know today, but it forms a fascinating period in the development of what has been called 'a nation of shopkeepers'.

kinds (not including beer, wine, or spirits) . . . it is desired to provide food and drink, thoroughly wholesome and well prepared, at a moderate cost, in order to meet the wants of a large population which now throngs the public houses in the neighbourhood. There is probably no district in London where more sin and distress are continually caused by intemperance . . .' Coffee and cocoa houses were also soon provided at railway stations 'for the convenience of passengers', and at other places; indeed it was reported that Mr Gladstone gave his support to the 'Coffee Tavern Movement'.

Toys and Toyshops

Before we look at toys and toyshops, during the Victorian period, we must recall the role of children at that time. In Cornwall, for instance, in the 1860s, boys as young as twelve worked nine or ten hours a day in the tin mines, even having their mid-day meal on site; for them there was little opportunity to play. Younger children might spend their time divided between attending school, helping with household chores or working part-time in low paid employment. Whenever they had any free time, in the evenings or on rare holidays, they would play outdoors with hoops, balls, skipping ropes, marbles or spinning tops. Girls played dancing or rhyming games, such as Oranges and Lemons or London Bridge and boys would climb trees, go fishing or play football or cricket.

In the countryside children would go looking for birds' nests or run about in the fields, later in the year gathering berries and hazel nuts, and in the winter skating, sledging or sliding.

Poor families wouldn't be able to afford many toys and any they could afford would be bought at penny bazaars, at market stalls, fairs or from itinerant pedlars. These pedlars were often called 'chapmen', which comes from the word cheap, and the small books which they sold became known as 'chapbooks'. They would also sell crudely made items such as rough wooden dolls, soldiers, or

cheap tin toys. Other toys might be home-made, perhaps a kite, a wooden cart or a doll. It was only at Christmas that such children might have received more expensive toys, such as those given out at parties organized by the local gentry or clergy.

However, before 1837 German toy whole-salers in Nuremberg were issuing illustrated catalogues, and over 1,200 items are listed in one early one. Today we may be surprised to discover that popular toys from the early part of this century were already available at the beginning of Queen Victoria's reign, including kaleido-scopes and strobo-scopes (where a cardboard disc with figures drawn on it was rotated quickly in front of a mirror, and gave the impression that the figure was moving).

FACING PAGE, LEFT: *A Victorian child's Christmas wish.*
FACING PAGE, RIGHT: *A contemporary advertisement showing the ever popular sledge made from a Sunlight soap box.*
ABOVE: *A tempting advertisement featured in* The Graphic *in time for Christmas 1888.*
RIGHT: *Lowther Arcade, London depicted by Thomas Crane,* London Town, *1833.*

In London a number of toy shops came into existence in the mid to late nineteenth century. William Hamley, who was born in 1803, took over the Toy Warehouse at 231 High Holborn in 1830. It became known as the 'Noah's Ark' because this was one of the main toys it sold, and being a toy based on a Bible story, it could be played with on a Sunday. For many years the shop used the Noah's Ark as a symbol and had one displayed over the door. Hamleys always aimed to sell the very best and other toys included tin soldiers, rag dolls, hoops and wooden hobby horses. About 1861 it acquired Blands of 35 New Oxford Street, a celebrated conjuring and magical business, and by 1875 Hamleys had opened a branch at 12 Oxford Street and later on at 64 Regent Street.

From the pages of a letter, in the ownership of the family, we get a brief glimpse of William Henry Hamley, son of William, in the closing years of the century. Each day he would ride to the shop on a bus and 'I can see now Mr Wm

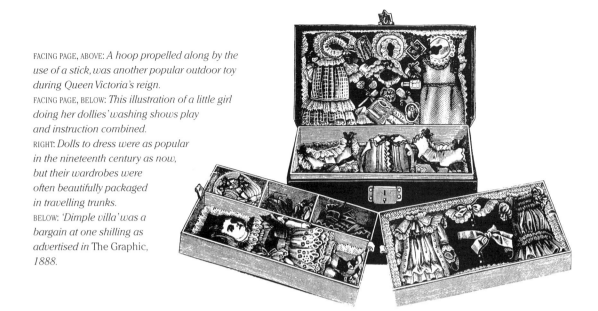

FACING PAGE, ABOVE: *A hoop propelled along by the use of a stick, was another popular outdoor toy during Queen Victoria's reign.*
FACING PAGE, BELOW: *This illustration of a little girl doing her dollies' washing shows play and instruction combined.*
RIGHT: *Dolls to dress were as popular in the nineteenth century as now, but their wardrobes were often beautifully packaged in travelling trunks.*
BELOW: *'Dimple villa' was a bargain at one shilling as advertised in* The Graphic, *1888.*

Hamley, always a flower in his coat. A florist in the Seven Sisters Road used to have one ready for him every morning.' The writer went on to describe one of the toys he remembered which Hamleys sold, called 'The Walking Postman': 'A postman pushing a parcel-post barrow. You held one wheel, with the other you wound up a piece of elastic and then put it on the ground. Result – in the unwinding of the elastic the truck moved along.'

As the years passed the range of toys increased to include dolls and games, wooden puzzles and also sports equipment. Ping Pong, an onomatopoeic name, was introduced exclusively through Hamleys as Queen Victoria's reign came to an end – it would be some years before it became known as Table Tennis. Unfortunately, also about this time, the original Noah's Ark premises were damaged by fire and in another letter we are reminded

of the circumstances: 'Up dashed a hansom cab [to Mr Hamley's home] and in it a porter from Holborn [from the shop]. No telephone in those days you know. [The porter] Rushed into the garden and shouted "Come on, sir, all the shop's on fire"... Off dashed your uncle and Mr Bilko in the waiting cab ... It [the fire] was luckily stopped in the basement and after it there was a marvellous sale of salvaged toys.'

C N Mackie's Magical Depot at the Pantheon in Oxford Street was a popular source for Christmas presents for they also sold conjuring tricks and boxes of puzzles. Other well-known toy shops in the latter part of the period included W H Cremer of 27 New Bond Street, Morrell's of Burlington Arcade, and J S Theobald & Co at the West End Manufactory in Kensington Church Street. Toys were also sold in shops which had a range of

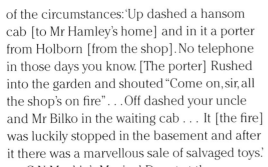

other goods, toys being only a small part of the trade, and in bazaars. The most famous of these was the Lowther Arcade where two rows of lock-up shops, almost all stocking toys, faced each other across a covered passage.

In the *Chambers' Journal* for 1889 a toy is defined as 'a trifling object, designed for the amusement of the young'. This was certainly true of the objects used as toys by the poor children, but not so for the children of richer households who had very elaborate playthings, many of them being smaller versions of items which taught children the work ethic. The same article reminds us that the toys of that period were 'so varied as to defy enumeration, and their rough classification is the most that can be attempted'. As today, many toys attempted to imitate real things – dogs, horses, babies, houses, windmills, boats – and in Victorian

FACING PAGE, ABOVE: *Two prints from a series entitled* Little Mothers *by Miss Emily Lees, the captions read: 'Just the image of his dear papa' and 'Now Geraldine Maude, Attend to me: I won't have any stuff about being married for love. It doesn't matter about Eliza, she's going to sell the "War Cry".' (1888).*
FACING PAGE BELOW AND THIS PAGE RIGHT: *A selection of typical toys for sale.* BELOW: *Toys were often sold in iron-mongers and other general emporia.*

times they were made of materials as varied as iron, wood, wax and india-rubber. In those days dolls had eyes that opened and closed (early ones operated by wires whilst later ones were counterweighted) and made noises that mimicked the words 'Mamma' or 'Papa', toy mice would run across the floor or monkeys climb up a pole.

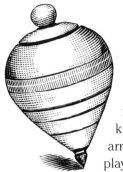

Other toys which were popular were those that encouraged the accomplishment of skills, such as making a top spin, flying a kite, building up bricks or arranging them into a picture, playing cards such as 'Happy Families', or kicking and throwing balls or rolling marbles. Of course we must not forget the toys which make a great noise, perhaps much to the annoyance of parents, such as pistols, drums and trumpets and, for babies, the simple rattle.

The manufacturing of toys in foreign countries, for export to Britain, was quite a large source of employment. In the years 1882–86 the average annual sum spent on toys imported into Britain was £579,629 – £320,000 on those from Germany, £90,000 from France, a smaller amount from Belgium and some from the United States, whilst £125,000-worth came from Holland. Indeed a couplet existed which said:

The children of Holland take pleasure in making,
What the children of England take pleasure in breaking.

This old rhyme related to the way in which wax and rag dolls, also known as Flander's

Babies, had for a long time been made by children in Holland, and were exported to Britain.

In Victorian times the English toymaker was often said to be not very enterprising, although in that same period we annually exported £60,000 worth of toys a year to Africa and South America. He was, however, very good at making wooden horses, particularly rocking-horses, which were frequently exported to Germany. Carts and other vehicles, drums and dolls' houses were generally made in London.

Many dolls were imported into Britain from France and Germany. The largest and cheapest doll manufactory in England was Thos Hatch's at 89 and 90 Long Lane, Smithfield, which also

ABOVE LEFT: *Spinning tops were popular for entertainment and developing skills.*

ABOVE RIGHT: *Many of the most expensive dolls were manufactured in France.*

BELOW: *The stone bricks in Richter's boxes were popular with both children and adults.*

FACING PAGE: *Playing cards and conjuring tricks were always acceptable presents for boys and girls. Dolls, animals on wheels and baby rattles also featured.*

made wax boys' and men's heads for tailors' busts. Many dolls' heads, from the middle of the nineteenth century, were made of unglazed porcelain, known as bisque, which was more life-like than glazed porcelain. The bodies, however, were far from life-like, but they were well-disguised by an array of fashionable clothes; the best examples of these were made in France. Many European baby dolls appear to have been influenced by earlier Japanese dolls. During the whole of the period dolls could be obtained which had 'speaking mechanisms'.

Building bricks, it seems, have always been popular with young children, be they empty packets or similar items found around the house, or ones with pictures or letters pasted on to the sides which could also be used in an educational manner. Some of the best-known bricks, or blocks, were those made in Rudolfstadt in Germany by F.Ad. Richter & Co, who also had premises in Railway Place, off Fenchurch Street in London. Their advertisement for 'Anchor Stone Building Boxes' in *The Graphic*, in January 1887, about nine years after their introduction to Britain, described them as 'The toy the Child likes best'. These coloured stones, formed from a mixture of sand, ground chalk, linseed oil, varnish and colour, were moulded into various shapes.

The firm was keen to point out that: 'Even grown-up people find pleasure in it. Indeed, many rich, aged gentlemen who have been given to weariness have expressed their gratitude for the agreeable occupation which has been afforded them by the magnificent large Boxes of Stone Bricks.' These blocks were available from toy-dealers, booksellers, stationers and educational depots throughout the country.

Other quiet activities included cutting out pictures – for instance, in 1865 children could cut

ROCKING HORSES, best finish in five sizes. Prices:—£1,
£2, £3, £4, and £5 each. Children's Carriages of superior elegance, and compact,
build, and so perfectly secure and easy that children may be trusted with impunity to the
most careless hands, £1 up to £20. Best Bagatelle Boards, all lengths, prices £2, £3, £4,
and £5 each. Child's Chairs from 3s. to 30s. each. Easy, Invalid, and In-and-out-door
Self-acting Wheel Chairs, on sale or hire. N.B. Rout Seats, Dining, Card, and Rout Tables lent for parties.—INGRAM'S Manufactory, 29, City-road, Finsbury-square, London.

LEFT. *England was and is justly proud of its rocking horses. (An early advertisement, 1844).*
BELOW: *Hinde's shilling toys of 1888, included dolls with full fashionable wardrobes.*
FACING PAGE, ABOVE: *The age of steam inspired beautiful model engines.*
BELOW: *'I'm just tinking [sic] where dolls go when they die'.*

out and make a model of the 'Monument of London'. Particular favourites were toy theatre sheets, from which characters could be cut, and made to stand up by means of slots in the base, for use in the family's model theatre.

Many books for children were regularly advertised in journals such as *The Illustrated London News*. There were play books for the nursery, which might take the form of indestructible illustrated large print books of *Easy*

known today for Dean's Rag Books, and Routledge, Warne and Routledge, whose early books were illustrated using hand-coloured wood-cuts, but later ones had large glossy pictures. Famous stories first published in the Victorian era include *Alice in Wonderland*, *The Wonderful Wizard of Oz*, and *Heidi*.

Words, *Easy Spelling*, or the *The Child's Own Alphabet*; these were published by Ward Lock. Similar books included *Nursery Rhymes*, *The Royal Picture Alphabet of Humour* and *Droll Moral Tales*, and *A Hundred Short Tales for Children*, the latter being translated from the German by the Rector of Woodchurch in Kent. These were all advertised in December 1859, as was *Kingston's Annual for Boys*, 1860, which cost six shillings and was described as the best present for a boy. It contained: '480 pages of interesting reading and 80 Illustrations. It is difficult to conceive how any volume could be made more attractive than this for the class for whom it is intended.' Other publishers included Dean and Son, better

From Small Acorns . . .

Many small businesses and shops took advantage of the development of better roads and the growth of the railways during the Victorian era. They expanded the area into which they sold their produce and gradually became either nationally, or internationally known. From what was originally a one-man shop, perhaps in the market area of an industrial city, grew an industry far beyond what the founder could ever have envisaged.

It was in 1847, in Newcastle-upon-Tyne, that William Owen opened a chemist's shop at Barras Bridge. As chemist's shops did, he stocked a thousand-and-one proprietary articles, but behind the shop he also had his own mineral water factory where he made soda water, seltzer, lemonade, ginger-beer and a sparkling tonic water; these he supplied in bottles and syphons. He was also an agent for many table waters, including Schweppes, and for several foreign mineral waters. The business developed a high reputation in Newcastle and the surrounding district and had a large and influential clientele. Today, though, he is remembered as the creator of Lucozade, which he first made for his sick daughter.

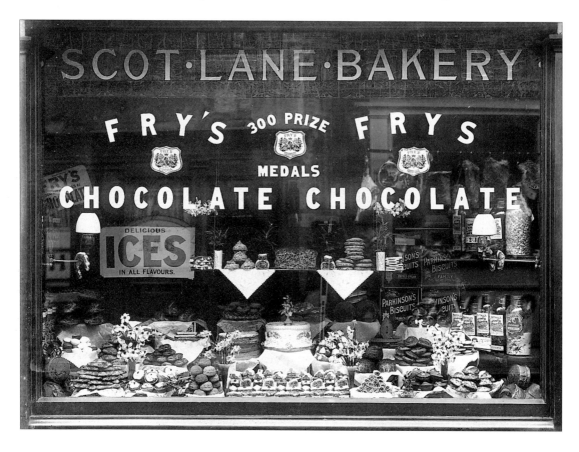

The centre of business life in Newcastle in the 1800s was the Groat Market, called by some the Meal Market. Here, among other things, were sold groats – oats with the hulls ground off – to make into meal. In this hub of activity were the usual inns and taverns – the Golden Lion, Unicorn, Fighting Cocks, and the Flying Horse (the latter was known locally as the notorious 'Hell's Kitchen' – here the great poker, used to prod the large open fire, was chained to the chimney to prevent the rather boisterous patrons from using it as a weapon to settle a dispute). Among the craftsmen who plied their trades, the glassblowers, the brass-founders, shoe-smiths, and gold-beaters, was another pharmacist, James Crossley Eno. His shop was quite distinctive for in the window stood three large flasks, one green, one red and one yellow – at night they were illuminated from behind by the gas jets in the pharmacy. He started his business in the 1850s, having served an apprenticeship with a pharmacist in the Sandhill district of the city.

At that time Newcastle was an important seaport with about 300 wooden sailing ships arriving with every tide. Life on the ships was

FACING PAGE: *Scot Lane Bakery window, Doncaster, Yorkshire, featuring Fry's Chocolate and Nuttall's rum and butter drops.*
RIGHT: *The Worcester Street premises 1847–87 of Alfred Bird and Sons.*

Mr Eno, however, found a way of relieving the suffering without inflicting more grief in the remedy – he created a clear sparkling tonic which he called Eno's Fruit Salt. As can be imagined its fame spread rapidly, whilst the other repulsive preparations declined in popularity. Not only was it popular in Newcastle but also in foreign ports, for Mr Eno had given a few spare packets of the white powder to some of the sea-captains who then became middlemen in a profitable trade. The captains started placing larger orders, for they were also selling it to merchants in these distant lands, and very soon the merchants were sending their orders

very hard, with poor food, little sleep and the influences of severe weather conditions, and when the sailors arrived in port they made up for these deprivations by over- indulging in food, drink and the high life! Such living caused indigestion, liverishness and related problems, and vile tasting preparations were swallowed to relieve the gross discomfort.

direct to the Newcastle pharmacy. As the business expanded Mr Eno decided to move to London, in the 1870s, and handed over his shop in Newcastle to his trusted apprentice George Heslop. In London's Pomeroy Street, at New Cross, he built a small factory; now he was able to dictate his own terms, insisting on cash with order and minimum orders of one gross.

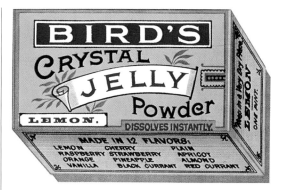

One day, in about 1835, Lord Sandys, who had been Governor of Bengal, walked into the shop and asked for a sauce to be made up for him

"Alas! my poor Brother"

Nevertheless, James Crossley Eno was a truly philanthropic man, giving away large sums of money both in his lifetime and also through his will. For instance, in 1889 Newcastle Infirmary was trying to raise £100,000 in order to inherit a similar sum bequeathed by John Hall, a shipping magnate; Eno gave £1,500, but when the organizer informed him of the fund's shortfall he wired back asking the amount of the shortfall and assuring the hospital that he would send the amount outstanding by return – it needed a further £8,500!

While Eno's Fruit Salt is the firm's most well-known preparation, it also made Anti-Bilious Pills, Digestive Granules, Solution of Roses, Iron and Quinine Tonic, Sugar Tablets, and Vegetable Moto.

Down in Worcester John Lea and William Perrins had a chemist's shop in Broad Street.

Worcester and then in 1897 they moved from their shop to a new factory in Midland Road. The recipe and the maturing time are both still secret, even today.

Down in the south west, in 1880, another famous product came into being, this time not in a chemist's shop but in a bakery.

from a recipe he had acquired in India – in those days chemists were also grocers and sellers of general provisions. When they made up the sauce they also made a few extra gallons of it with a view to assessing its commercial viability. This they poured into stone jars, but, on tasting it, they found it so unpalatable that they consigned it to the cellars.

Some time later they came upon the jars and before throwing them out decided to taste the sauce once again – it was superlative, the sauce had matured! They obtained permission from Lord Sandys to use the recipe and manufactured and sold it under the now familiar Lea & Perrins name as Worcestershire Sauce. In 1845 they opened a factory in Bank Street,

In Plymouth, a local physician, Dr William Penn Eales, had become concerned about the quality and cost of baby foods. This concern inspired him to develop a formula for a biscuit-like cereal which was pre-cooked at Farley's bakery and was originally known as Farley's Feeding Biscuits – today we know them as Farley's Rusks.

In Victorian times life was very much about work, at least for most people, but some were able to turn their enterprise into a hobby which others could enjoy. Edward Stanley Gibbons was one such person. He was born in Plymouth, where he joined his father in his pharmaceutical chemist's shop on the death of his elder brother. The world's first postage stamps were produced in 1840, the same year that Stanley Gibbons was born, and by about 1854 he had about twenty stamps in a small book.

Stamp collecting was just beginning and when there was

any spare time, in between making pills and potions, he concentrated on his new-found interest. It is said it was his father who first recognized the potential of dealing in stamps and he set aside a desk for Stanley in the shop exclusively for that purpose. As the new trade grew a room above the shop was made available and the business was called E S Gibbons, before becoming E Stanley Gibbons and, later still, Stanley Gibbons & Co.

When his father died Stanley Gibbons sold the pharmacy and concentrated on the sale of stamps. One morning in 1863 two sailors came into the shop with a kit-bag full of Cape of Good Hope triangular stamps and he gave them a £5 note for the lot. This purchase was indeed a stroke of good fortune and he calculated that this deal alone made him about £500! He started to import unused stamps from all over the world and his brother, who was a Commander in the

Royal Navy, also brought parcels of stamps back when he returned from his voyages.

In 1865 Stanley Gibbons issued a monthly price list, the prototype of the now famous Gibbons Stamp Catalogues, and in about 1870 he published his first stamp album. In 1874 he moved to London and his business became almost entirely conducted by correspondence, handling 200 to 300 letters a day. He was able to retire in 1890, a rich man, one who had developed a boyhood interest into a business; almost single-handed he had created a hobby that would, for many people, become an all-absorbing passion. He sold the business to Charles J Phillips for £25,000, this being Phillips's valuation of the stock, and then remained as chairman of the new company. In 1891 the business was moved to half a shop at 435 Strand, before later moving to its world famous address – 391 Strand.

For most people, however, business involved life's essentials – clothing, coal, machinery,

agriculture, transportation, shop-keeping and, within the latter, food. It was in Manchester's Market Street, opposite the Royal Exchange, that the 24-year-old Arthur Brooke opened his shop. Market Street was always busy as housewives looked for bargains and above his door he put the sign 'Brooke, Bond & Co.' – but there never was a Mr Bond. Arthur Brooke said the name 'seemed to him to sound well'! He sold tea, coffee and

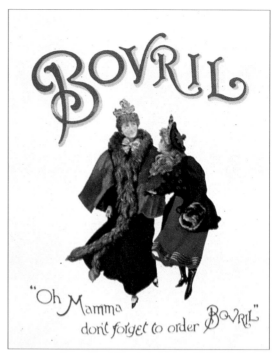

"Oh Mamma don't forget to order Bovril"

"Say Guard! Am I right for BOVRIL"

sugar – but only for cash; he was a great salesman: his teas were always reliable and he developed his own blends, always packed to give full weight, and described as 'Deliciously Rich', 'Ripe, Juicy', 'Fragrant' and 'the Crème de la Crème'.

His business prospered and soon he opened shops in Liverpool, Leeds and Bradford, taking over a warehouse in London in 1872. However, in the late 1870s there was a trade depression which particularly affected the industrial north of England. Typical of the man, Arthur Brooke's first action was to reduce his own standard of living by selling his house and giving up his carriage and horses.

A retail grocer asked if he might buy Brooke Bond's blended tea in bulk at wholesale prices. Arthur realized that other grocers might also be interested and he started advertising wholesale supplies of blended tea, but, as always, it had to be cash with the order. Orders came flooding in and in 1892 the firm became Brooke Bond & Co Ltd. Now the business had become primarily wholesale. He believed in three basic factors – intelligent buying, sensible blending and clever advertising – and they were to give his company a national reputation. In the *Yorkshireman* in 1893, for instance, the company advertised 'It's Here! The New Season's Tea has arrived! This appetising announcement excites a thrill of expectant pleasure in millions of minds. It's an annual event welcomed eagerly by English womankind especially. What longing for the fresh and fragrant leaf! *Brooke Bond's New Tea* is undoubtedly the very best. Brisk, flavoury, refreshing, it's just the cup to comfortably revive and cheer you in these drowsy August days.'

Scotland has long been renowned for its tasty fare, its haggis, oatcakes and biscuits. Robert McVitie was born in 1809. He grew up in Dumfries, serving an apprenticeship with a Scottish baker before setting up in business in Rose Street, Edinburgh in 1830 as a high-quality retail baker and confectioner. As the business

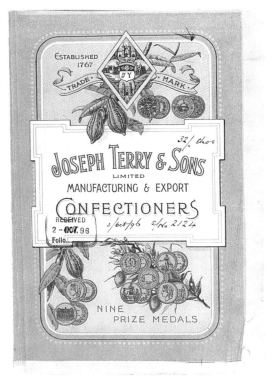

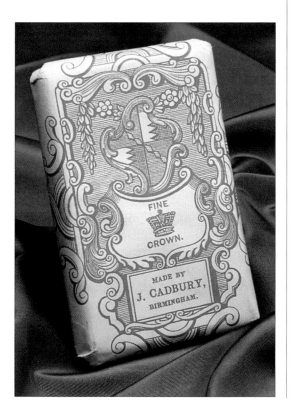

expanded he opened branches in various parts of the city.

After his son, also Robert, had served his apprenticeship he went to France and Austria to study baking and confectionery. On his return the younger Robert set about the further expansion of the business not only in Scotland, but also in England. In those days bread did not keep very long, and as an alternative they produced biscuits for long distance customers.

One day in 1887 Alexander Grant marched into the shop, having seen a display of scones in the shop window. He wanted to tell Robert McVitie that he could make better ones than those – he went on to prove the point, and also joined the firm! The following year Charles Price, one of the company's salesmen became a partner and the company became McVitie & Price.

In 1892 it was the same Alexander Grant who created the first Digestive biscuit, originally

the present day, their name lives on in products consumed in many homes across the British Isles.

Also up in Scotland, George Baxter opened a grocer's shop in Spey Street, Fochabers. Previously he had been one of fifty gardeners on the Castle Gordon Estate, midway between Aberdeen and Inverness. George's wife, Margaret, was an excellent cook and in the back of the shop she made her jellies and jams. Visitors to the area, and especially the shooting and fishing party guests of the Duke of Richmond and Gordon, bought her specialities with great enthusiasm. So greatly did they enjoy them that they wrote from their homes ordering further supplies, and

so-called because it contained baking soda – a product known to help control flatulence; indeed it was a 'medicinal' ingredient felt to aid the digestive system. In 1893 the firm was commissioned to provide a wedding cake for the marriage of the Duke of York and Princess Mary (later King George V and Queen Mary), a tradition which was to continue for many generations. The firm may no longer be shopkeepers but throughout Victorian times, and to

so the business spread throughout the country. George and Margaret's son, William, joined the small family business and travelled by train to the distant corners of Scotland, taking with him his bicycle; as he cycled back he collected orders. By early in the twentieth century the business had grown so much a new jam factory was needed, and the company's growth must now have exceeded George's wildest dreams.

Another man with enthusiasm and initiative was Alfred Bird who opened a small shop in Bell Street, Birmingham in 1837, beneath the old Market Hall. He was a Fellow of the Chemists Society and outside his shop he put up the sign 'Alfred Bird F.C.S. – Experimental Chemist'. We are told that whilst he would no doubt make and sell many of the popular medicinal and toiletry preparations of his day he most of all enjoyed the hours he spent in the back room of the shop, after the customers had gone, and here he experimented. Not least was his hope of finding something which his wife could eat and enjoy for she had an intolerance to yeast-based prod-ucts, which of course included bread, and also had what we would call an allergy to eggs, which meant that although she liked custard, she could not enjoy it.

In 1843 he perfected a yeast substitute, which he called Birds Fermenting Powder, and which was later called Baking Powder. He also created an eggless custard – he did the impos-sible, for the dictionary states that custard is a mixture of eggs and milk – using cornflour. His name was to become synonymous with the product, which was to be the foundation of a new business.

In 1837 the London-Birmingham railway was completed and by 1850, with the company now in larger premises in Worcester Street, Alfred Bird was sending his products to all parts of Great Britain where they were found on the shelves of many grocers' shops.

Today we recognize his contribution to convenience foods mainly through these two products, but he also invented another commercially viable proposition, a perpetually

HOVIS
FORMS GOOD
BONE, BRAIN, FLESH AND MUSCLE.

HOVIS BUILDS UP STRONG MEN.

burning nightlight, which could be safely replenished with oil while it was still alight.

Alfred Bird believed in advertising and is credited as being the first to give advertising calendars away free. His business, rather like a church, had an exhortatory motto on an inside wall to encourage workers to greater efforts:

> Early to Bed Early to rise
> Stick to your Work . . . And Advertise

Eventually the firm became Alfred Bird & Sons. His eldest son, Alfred Frederick Bird, brought new drive to the business and he introduced what might be called an early example of a marketing and sales promotion policy.

In 1848 he had issued an almanack, and in 1855 he took his first small advertising space in the *Illustrated London News*. Four years later he issued an elaborate full colour lithographic

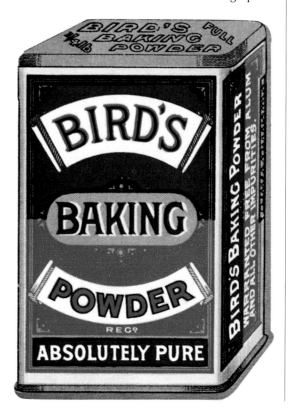

print showing Bird's Custard Powder being used on the historic Franklin Expedition.

Another new product, launched in the 1870s, was Bird's Blancmange Powder, which created a novel cold dessert in no less than fourteen flavours! It was immediately popular. Alfred Bird died in 1879, but Alfred jnr was already a dominant figure and in 1880 the company started to produce its first pictorial advertisements, the beginning of many famous designs which included such well-known captions as: 'When the pie was opened the birds began to sing the praises of Bird's Custard'.

Sadly in 1887, Queen Victoria's Jubilee year, his factory was burnt to the ground, said to have been as a result of a firework-throwing crowd celebrating the Jubilee, and he had to start again. More new products came forward including Bird's Egg Substitute and Bird's Jelly Crystals, the forerunner of the jelly tablet we know today.

In 1876 the firm's first trademark, 'The Ship on the World' had been registered, but it wasn't until the end of the Queen's reign that the largest change took place – in 1900 Alfred Bird & Sons Limited was formed, but it was still like a family business for Alfred Frederick Bird was appointed chairman and managing director and his sons became members of the board.

Taking Home the Groceries

Thomas Lipton was born in 1850 and on his twenty-first birthday he opened his little shop in Stobcross Street, Glasgow – it bore the name 'Lipton's Market'. His shop was beautifully clean and his white apron was testimony to the care he took to ensure everything was hygienic and in good order. His aim was 'Better value for money': better bacon, cheese and eggs, as well as a wide range of other products, and all at lower prices than those charged by other shops.

BELOW: The historic visit of Henry Heinz to Fortnum & Mason which resulted in his products being sold there to the present day.

As his policies succeeded he opened further and larger shops; by 1876 he had twenty, and by 1898 he had two hundred shops, spread all over the British Isles. To enable him to offer his lower prices he had developed a policy of buying direct from Irish farmers and crofters, often visiting them in their homes and paying cash for all he bought. We are told that on one occasion he even pawned his watch as he did not have enough money to pay a farmer.

Most people take milk with their tea and in 1874 Provincial Dairies was established in the heart of Leeds to supply dairy produce to city dwellers at a moderate price. The premises on

Park Lane consisted of a 'handsome shop' and warehouse. Even in the 1890s it had electric lighting, not least because 'this light is better adapted to the requirements of the dairy trade, being cooler and cleaner than gas'. Later it opened premises in Upperhead Row, on the corner of busy Briggate, where the shop had a frontage of fifteen feet. Inside it had marble and carved oak panels, which had artistic representations of cows, poultry, etc; there were also marble topped counters and a tessellated floor of coloured blocks. Not only did Provincial Dairies cater for individual shoppers but it also supplied hotels and restaurants in the city. The firm was proud to boast that pure new milk and nursery milk were supplied twice daily and that it 'is subject to frequent and careful chemical analysis'.

Down in London some twenty years earlier two young apprentices had joined the firm of West & Wyatt which supplied oils used in sauces; the two apprentices were Edmund Crosse and Thomas Blackwell. They quickly formed a bond and when William Wyatt decided to retire in 1829 the two young men, still in their mid-twenties, bought the business. After a further nine years they acquired premises at 21 Soho Square which became both their factory and shop and they built a house on the site, the two families living above the shop. Although very poor in those early years, by 1844 they had increased their capital to £25,000, and in that year they made a profit of £5,000. From as early as 1837 they became Royal Warrant holders and throughout the world their name is connected with soups and sauces. Crosse and Blackwell are

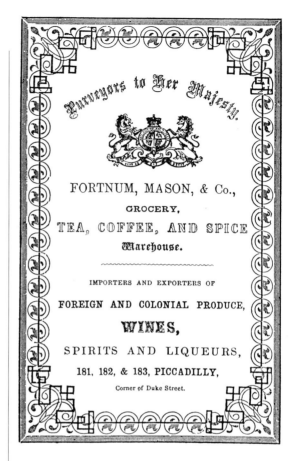

described in 1859 as 'Purveyors in Ordinary to her Majesty', and were 'inviting attention to their pickles, sauces, tart fruits, and other table delicacies, the whole of which are prepared with the most scrupulous attention to wholesomeness and purity'.

While Crosse & Blackwell may have been an early name in the production of soups and sauces it was an American, Henry Heinz, who was to dominate the market place later in Victoria's reign. In June 1886 Henry J Heinz made his historic visit to Fortnum & Mason in London's Piccadilly, probably Britain's best-known grocery store and purveyor of groceries to Queen Victoria. Heinz, resplendent in top hat and frock coat and bristling with energy, asked for the head of grocery purchasing, saying he had brought with him, from America 'seven varieties of our finest and newest goods'.

Mason had a small shop in St James's Market. In 1756 the firm moved to 183 Piccadilly where, along with adjoining properties, it still trades today. By the time Queen Victoria came to the throne the company was already well established.

The firm's ready-to-eat dishes became very popular with those organizing the catering at some of the large events which attracted vast numbers of overseas visitors, events such as the Coronation and the Great Exhibition of 1851, as well as the Boat Race, Ascot, Lords, Henley Regatta, and Cowes.

During her reign the store held Warrants of Appointment not only from Queen Victoria, but also from the Prince and Princess of Wales, the Duke of Edinburgh, their Royal Highnesses Prince and Princess Christian of Schleswig-Holstein, and the Crown Princess of Prussia (who was also Princess Royal of Great Britain and Ireland). Indeed Queen Victoria sent 250lbs of Fortnum & Mason's concentrated beef tea to Scutari in the Crimea for Florence Nightingale's use in the hospitals.

Beef tea was also a popular drink in many households in this country, but during the latter part of the nineteenth century its nutritious

After tasting each one, the head of grocery purchasing gave his famous reply, 'I think, Mr Heinz, we will take the lot.'

It was Henry Heinz who created the slogan '57 varieties'. The first Heinz baked beans, with their tomato sauce, were produced in 1895 – originally they also contained a piece of pork, but this was later discontinued.

What of Fortnum & Mason themselves? William Fortnum had royal connections for he was a footman in the Royal Household of Queen Anne. Hugh

value was challenged by the introduction of Johnston's Fluid Beef. Advertisements claimed that one ounce of this gave more direct nourishment than fifty ounces of ordinary meat extract. Johnston set up a factory in London, after his Canadian one burnt down, and started to market his Bo Vril, even selling it in public houses. The first records of sales of Bovril drink are for 1886, and there were free tastings at the Colonial and Continental Exhibition in South Kensington. In 1890 the programme for the St James's Theatre in London presents Lily Langtry in *As You Like It* – and 'at all the bars of this theatre' Bovril and Bovril ices; at one stage it was also possible to buy Bovril chocolate from slot machines! Many of the early advertisements for Bovril were to last for years and are still famous today, such as W H Caffyn's poster 'Alas! my poor brother'. Perhaps the manufacturers could rightly claim it to be 'the food product of the Victorian era'. The outbreak of the Boer War, in 1899, where death was a poignant concern, was reflected in advertising that Bovril was 'liquid life at the front'.

It might be said that selling groceries is 'money-for-jam'; it certainly was to become so for one man. William Pickles Hartley's family were grocers at Waterside on the outskirts of Colne, Lancashire but he wanted to become a pharmacist when he left school. Unfortunately that was not possible and he joined the family business, developing its wholesale potential. He

LEFT: *Small grocers also flourished although they were often family firms as this painting,* Grocer and Wife, *1868, by Charles Green depicts.*
FACING PAGE, ABOVE: *A modern photograph of a Penrith Market Square shop well known throughout the Victorian era.*
FACING PAGE, BELOW: *Fresh produce was available from street vendors.*

regularly walked across the rugged Pennine moors to Haworth and neighbouring villages, so well known to the Brontë sisters, to gain orders from the small shop-keepers. It was as a result of difficulties in obtaining supplies from jam manufacturers that the Hartleys started making their own. William, a strongly active Primitive Methodist, who was appointed organist at the Waterside chapel at the age of thirteen, even before he had learnt to play, had to leave all this behind when, in 1874, he moved to Bootle to become a jam manufacturer.

Twice his factory had to be extended. He was considered an ideal employer, one who raised wages without pressure, provided dining rooms where cost price meals could be obtained, provided homes with gardens to rent or buy, and, early in the twentieth century, introduced a profit sharing scheme for his workers, 'not because it pays commercially . . . but because it seems to me right'. He liked to claim that wherever possible the fruit was picked, made into jam and put into earthenware jars during the same day. He started making mar-

malade to fill that period of the year when other fruits were not available, thus obviating the laying off of staff. The name of Hartley's jam became known throughout England, especially after he opened a factory in London, and is still sold today.

Many smaller grocers would stock products like those made by William Hartley, and John Rowntree & Sons of Scarborough was no doubt one of them. The family business had been founded early in the nineteenth century and towards the end of the century had shops in both Westborough and Newborough Street.

Its 'judicious management' carried 'varied and carefully selected stocks of groceries and other products which were well arranged, a fine display of leading specialities being always visible in the large and lofty plate glass windows'. The firm bought when prices were favourable and always had plenty of reserve

stocks, which enabled it to execute large orders. Its own tea department blended teas purchased from India, China and Ceylon, and it also carried 'pure and high class coffee'. Rowntrees also had cafés in the shop in Westborough and the Grand Hall of The Spa.

In the same seaside town Henry Wellburn had started business in 1812 but during Queen Victoria's reign he became a leading supplier of groceries, general provisions and Italian goods. He also started to import wines, spirits and liqueurs and at that time had stocks from Hungary and Australia as well as the normal range of wines from France, Germany and Spain. Wellburns were also the oldest ale and porter bottlers in the town.

Across in Huddersfield, towards the end of the century, Foster's Cash Stores was advertising that it sold finest malt vinegar in 5, 12½, 25, and 50-gallon casks – warranted absolutely pure. It stocked superior candied peels, lemon, citron and orange; and also Cheshire and American cheese, as well as choice currants, sultanas, Valencias, Muscatels, figs, almonds, etc. Its slogan said that it was:

The Cheapest Shop for the Poor.
The Best Shop for the Rich.
The Right Shop for Everybody.
Buy at Foster's and Save Money.

Goodall, Backhouse & Co in Leeds manufactured many 'World Renowned Household Specialities', all no doubt regarded as a boon to the housewife. Its 'Yorkshire Relish', described as 'The most Delicious Sauce in the World', has had a reputation across the county until recent times. Additionally in 1888 it advertised: 'Goodall's Egg Powder – one sixpenny tin will go as far as 20 eggs'; Goodall's Baking Powder – Indispensable. Makes Puddings without Eggs, Pastry without Butter, and Bread without Yeast'; 'Goodall's Mushroom Ketchup – A full and rich flavoured Ketchup, unrivalled for its great strength, perfect purity, and unsurpassed flavour'; 'Goodall's Ginger Beer Powder – Makes three Gallons of the Best Ginger Beer in the world for threepence'; 'Goodall's Quinine Wine – The best remedy known for indigestion, General Debility, etc. Restores delicate individuals to health and vigour.' If readers of their advertisements wrote to Goodall, Backhouse & Co, enclosing a penny stamp for postage, the firm offered to present

them with a 104-page fully illustrated book of household recipes.

In 1869 Colman's reminded shoppers that 'Colman's British Corn-flour is prepared from Rice, the Staple Food of more than Three Hundred Millions (300,000,000) of People, and is unequalled for Blanc-Mange, Custards, Puddings, Cakes, Soups, &c. and is the most wholesome and easily digestible Food for Children and Invalids.' On the same page Brown and Polson's advertisement, twice the size of Colman's, simply stated that 'Brown and Polson's Corn Flour Is Genuine, Prepared solely from Maize – Indian Corn.' Similarly Hugon's extolled the virtues of its Refined Beef Suet (Atora Brand) over suet obtained from the butcher, and drew attention to the 'unnecessary trouble in stringing and chopping' ordinary suet as opposed to being able to use Atora 'at a moment's notice'.

'Specialities' of the day included one created in Paris by Englishman John Osborne, originally known as Patum Peperium. It was a pâté made from anchovy, butter, herbs and spices which was spread thickly on hot toast. Following the death of John Osborne in 1865, his son Charles moved to London and continued to make the delicacy which later became known as 'Gentleman's Relish'.

Then, of course, there was Lea & Perrins Worcestershire Sauce, made to Lord Sandy's recipe, and another recipe said to have been given to an English aristocrat was the one for Earl Grey Tea. Tradition has it that the formula was given to the 2nd Earl Grey (1764–1845) by a celebrated Chinese Mandarin. For many years this blend has been associated with the

Magazine of 1867 is 'supposed to be derived from the name of an Indian fruit, not unlike an orange, called the Aegle marmelos, or Indian Bael, from which at one time a similar conserve seems to have been made'.

James Robertson opened his grocery shop in Paisley in 1864. He was persuaded by a salesman to buy a barrel of bitter oranges, but as sales were very slow and the fruit needed to be disposed of quickly, Marion his wife suggested that she make them into marmalade. The demand exceeded all their expectations. Marion Robertson is credited with coining the name 'Golden Shred'; later this was followed by 'Silver Shred' for lemon marmalade.

Jackson family of Piccadilly, who have links with the area dating back to the end of the seventeenth century. Robert Jackson & Company was formed in the early part of the nineteenth century and became well known as Jacksons of Piccadilly; it is believed that the secret of the original blend was entrusted to one of the partners in 1830.

Often when tea is taken at breakfast it is accompanied by toast and marmalade. The word 'Marmalade', according to the *People's*

Scotland seems to have been the home of marmalade in Victorian times. Keiller's, in Dundee, employed 400 people and used 1½ million jars every year, which were specially made for them in the Potteries. Three thousand tons of bitter oranges were imported from Seville in Spain as the ones grown around that city 'possess a peculiar and agreeable aroma'. The whole of Keiller's production was carried out between the beginning of December and the end of March, over 1,000 tons annually.

Even in the 1850s tea and sugar were still quite costly and were treated with respect, hence the beautifully made tea-caddies and sugar basins we still see displayed today.

Henry Tate, at the age of thirteen, in 1832, went to Liverpool to enter the grocery trade. His brother, Caleb Ashworth Tate, was already in the city and it is probable Henry became an apprentice to his brother for seven years. At the age of twenty he acquired the business of Aaron Wedgewood in the Old Haymarket, in Liverpool, and became a master grocer, changing the name over the shop to 'Henry Tate'. By 1855 he had six shops, four in Liverpool, one in Ormskirk and the other in Birkenhead, and from such a beginning he entered the wholesale trade.

Then apparently he became restless and decided to become involved in sugar refining. It was a competitive industry and he had no experience in it, but in 1859 he became a partner in the firm of John Wright & Co of Liverpool. Nevertheless he retained his interest in his grocery business for a while, no doubt wanting to be sure he had made the correct decision.

In 1869 the partnership with John Wright was dissolved and Henry took his sons into the business,

which became Henry Tate & Sons. He built the Love Lane Refinery in Liverpool in 1870 and opened the Thames Refinery at Silvertown in 1878. Henry Tate died in 1899, and the amalgamation with Abram Lyle's company did not take place until 1921.

We know a little of the inside of the shop at Birkenhead for it was preserved much as Henry Tate built it, until the early 1950s. His method of taking cash is interesting. A small oblong section of the mahogany counter was removed and a glass panel put in its place; below the glass was a ledge, and underneath was the cash drawer. The customer's money was dropped

through a slot in the counter and fell on to the ledge, where it could be seen by both the customer and the shop assistant – there was no argument as to what monies had been offered, and then the coins later dropped into the cash drawer. There was also a counting house, where Henry wrote up his books, with a little window through which he could watch everything that was going on in the shop. In the cellar was the machine he used for crushing sugar-loaves, the type of machine he would later make obsolete when he became a joint licensee of the Langen patent for making cube sugar. On 31 December 1861 he made up his books for the last time, his twenty-nine years in the grocery trade had come to an end – now it was sugar.

At that time sugar, in the form of sugar crystals and syrup, was run off into clay cone-shaped moulds, each one holding from 5 to 35 pounds. The sugar-loaves were broken into small pieces by the grocer, using a chopping machine which often sat on the counter, or in some instances it was a treadle type, before the sugar was sold to the housewife. Sometimes the lumps were still too large for domestic use and

households had 'sugar nippers', smaller utensils, for reducing the sugar for table or cooking uses; when sifted sugar was required the sugar was broken down with a mortar. The sugar lump did not appear until about 1870.

As sugar needed refining, so did tea, for the early teas were of the large leaf variety.

In 1859 'Horniman's Pure Tea' is advertised in the classified advertisements of *The Illustrated London News*: 'The Lancet (p318) states of H & Co's Tea:-"The green, not being covered with Prussian Blue, is a dull olive: the black is not intensely dark. Wholesome and good tea is thus secured."'

Back in 1820 William Sumner took over a grocery and druggist's shop at the top of Birmingham's Bull Ring. In 1852 we find in Slater's *Directory of Birmingham* William Sumner & Son as tea and coffee dealers, but in 1860 William handed the business over to his two sons, John and William. Their 'Almanack' for that year lists a remarkable range of stock for a provincial shop of the period.

The brothers' partnership lasted until 1863 when William took his father's old Chemist and

Druggist's shop at 97 High Street, Birmingham and John took the Grocer's and Tea Dealer's at 98 High Street, a shop they had bought some years earlier. Tea was now an article of such large and general consumption that he was buying tea in both India and China and bringing to Birmingham a rich variety of samples, such as 'Finest Lapsang Souchong, Finest Kaisow, Finest Moning Congous, Green Teas, Assam, Oolong and Scented Teas.

However it was in a new century, and under a new monarch, that their name became really famous – when they created 'Typhoo Tipps Tea'.

Another essential commodity for the rich, but rarely affordable by the working classes, was butter. Not all butter, even in Victorian times, was home produced, for in *Chambers's Journal* in 1893 we read that the P & O Steamer *Ballarat* had brought to London 670 tons of butter from factories in Victoria and New South Wales, Australia. It was anticipated that a similar trade in Australian cheese might begin

and it was questioned why British farmers could not keep their butter through the winter when such ships could bring their produce through the tropics on its way to Britain.

Similarly, beef was brought to this country from Canada, consignments having come since a small landing in 1874, whilst mutton from New Zealand was arriving in such perfect condition, due to refrigeration, that butchers often passed it off as British.

RIGHT: *Wright's grocery store and post office, Catherine Street, Doncaster, by Luke Bagshaw.*

Making a House a Home

Once again we are faced with the different standards of living of the various strata of society in Victorian times. The poor people in their hovel had little room for furniture, nor could they afford much, and often their living room was also their work room. For instance, a hand weaver's loom might have to be in the same room in which the family slept.

In contrast, higher up the social scale, the house of the artisan, the tradesman or the works manager would be almost overfilled with belongings, especially as the era moved nearer to the time of the Queen's jubilees.

However, homes still lacked many of the amenities we take for granted today, and keeping them warm and clean cannot have been easy, although quite a lot of people in Victorian times had servants to do many of these tasks.

Magazines of the period give us a clear insight into Victorian homes, their advertisements being particularly detailed. Often these were for goods available from local shops or from the works of the manufacturers.

Heal's of Tottenham Court Road expanded with Victoria's reign. John Harris Heal started in business as a feather dresser in Rathbone Place but moved the firm to 203 Tottenham Court Road in 1818, a road soon to be known as the 'Furnishing Street of London'. At this stage he was described as a 'Mattress and Feather-Bed Manufacturer'. In 1840, after the death of her husband, the firm became Fanny

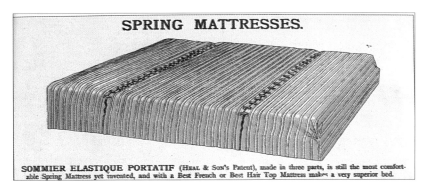

SPRING MATTRESSES.

SOMMIER ELASTIQUE PORTATIF (HEAL & SON's Patent), made in three parts, is still the most comfortable Spring Mattress yet invented, and with a Best French or Best Hair Top Mattress makes a very superior bed.

FACING PAGE: *An early advertisement for the use of Sunlight soap in every household.*
RIGHT: *Original illustrations from the famous Heal's, manufacturers of hand-made beds and mattresses.*
BELOW: *Hampton & Sons' London furniture store.*

Heal & Son and moved to 196 Tottenham Court Road, where a bedding factory was built; in 1847 the name was shortened to Heal & Son. John Harris Heal jnr, recognizing the importance of advertisements, placed them in the Charles Dickens novels, which were then being published in monthly instalments – he used seven of the novels and these advertisements ran for twenty-eight years! He also used advertising bills on railway station platforms, and realized the importance of the railway in delivering to his mail order customers.

Initially he supplied only bedding but later also sold wood and metal bedsteads as well as a range of other furniture. His 1852 catalogue listed 67 patterns of iron and brass bedsteads, which were popular as it was said that bed bugs and lice could not scale the slippery legs! However, it also listed mahogany four-poster and half-tester beds. The base of the bed was

generally a straw palliasse, although in 1860 he patented 'Le Sommier Elastique Portatif', a spring mattress which folded up into three sections for ease of handling and cleaning. The actual 'bedding' could be made of fine fleece, horsehair, white goose feathers or a combination of materials, depending on what money was to be spent.

Within forty years of opening in Tottenham Court Road, Heal's shop was one of the largest in London, and later a cabinet making workshop was also added.

In 1859 the firm was already offering a 'New Illustrated Catalogue' which contained 'designs and prices of 150 articles of Bedroom Furniture, as well as over 100 Bedsteads, and prices of every description of bedding'. Heal's also initiated the idea of creating a series of small rooms within the shop where customers could see how the furniture would look in their own home. As the century progressed the company increased its range and in 1880 introduced a department for sitting room furniture.

In the latter half of the 1860s the company expanded into an export trade with India, China and the colonies, but this was discontinued after a short time.

Ambrose Heal entered the business in 1893 and within a few years was making a significant contribution to the design of furniture, creating the Heal Style of hand-made items – he aimed to offer good design at reasonable prices, made from the finest materials. The 'Newlyn' and 'St. Ives' ranges of bedroom furniture, first offered in 1897, were made in fumed oak with wrought-steel handles and hinges. The following year some items made of mahogany with pewter inlay were also produced. The dressing-table mirror bore the motto: 'If this be vanity who'd be wise' and the wardrobe: 'Fine feathers make fine birds'. Some members of the furniture trade thought his designs were unsaleable, but his father allowed him a small part of the shop to display his work. Through exhibiting at the Arts & Crafts Exhibition he obtained an order

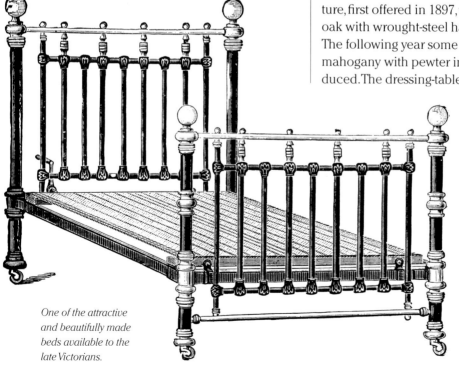

One of the attractive and beautifully made beds available to the late Victorians.

to supply the furniture and furnishings for the Hotel Standard at Norrkopping in Sweden in 1899. The following year he exhibited a bedroom at the Paris Exhibition.

Eventually the firm realized the need to supply furniture for the whole house and started to make beds and other items suitable for the servants' quarters as well as for the family.

Another well-known name, also to be found on Tottenham Court Road, was that of Maples. On 16 April 1841, John Maple opened his shop at Number 145, a most convenient

MAPLE & CO
Tottenham-court-road, London, W.
THE LARGEST AND MOST CONVENIENT
FURNISHING ESTABLISHMENT IN THE WORLD.
COMPLIMENTARY PRESENTS AND JUBILEE GIFTS.

NOVELTIES in Fancy DRAWING-ROOM FURNITURE, such as Brackets, Occasional Tables, Settees, Pouffe Ottomans, Gossip-Chairs, Card-Tables, Easels, Pedestals, Cabinets, Screens, Writing-Tables, &c., at most Moderate Prices. Special Catalogue. MAPLE and CO., London, Paris, and Smyrna.

THE BUXTON SUITE, 24 Guineas.

The BUXTON Drawing-room Suite, comprising a comfortable Couch, two Easy and six Occasional Chairs, upholstered in fashionable Tapestry or Velvet; a handsome Cabinet, with carved panels to lower doors, and cupboard above inclosed by bevelled plate-glass doors; elegant Overmantel, with seven bevelled silvered plates; and Octagonal Centre Table. Walnut or Ebonised, 24 Guineas.

place, for it was at the junction with New Road, later to become Euston Road; Tottenham Court Road formed an artery running north and south whilst New Road ran east to west. To the north and west of the site stretched green fields but soon these were to be part of the growing city – John Maple had envisaged this development, and the subsequent growth of his business. Initially the firm was Maple & Cook, Cook being Maple's brother-in-law, but he left within the first year. In addition to the name, up went the 'Hen and Chickens', the traditional sign of a draper.

In those early days customers could buy stair carpet at 6d a yard, drawing-room chairs at 2s 6d each, or a mahogany four-poster bed-stead for £2. Gas jets flickered in the shop and in the windows, illuminating the wealth of goods packing the still small premises.

Gradually the business at 145 Tottenham Court Road spread to the adjacent properties, 146 and 147, eventually becoming the largest furnishing house in the world. Not only did it sell furniture but also carpets and other household goods, and quality and value were its watchwords.

By the 1880s Maples covered a site which had previously been occupied by 200 houses – it was one of the sights of London and an attraction for American visitors to the capital. The company was also now a Royal Warrant Holder to the sovereign, as upholsterers.

In 1891 Maple & Co became a private limited company. Its catalogue of the following year contained 650 pages and the showrooms featured a selection of the rooms likely to be found in the homes of clients – library, billiard room, drawing room and dining room, vestibule, boudoirs and bedrooms, and even a Japanese room. The firm not only supplied the furniture and furnishings but would also carry out any other work required to make a house a home.

Waring's (later to become Waring & Gillow) of Oxford Street, London had furniture on display for normal trading, but also used the premises to house exhibitions of exquisite old embroideries alongside examples of modern British-made copies of important Italian furnishings. No doubt they intended that visitors to this free exhibition would purchase from their range of quality goods.

Some firms were keen to point out that their furniture was designed by artists and made by craftsmen; another emphasized the 'Cheapest and Best Bedstead ever offered' – in 1899 this consisted of a 3ft by 6ft 6in bedstead, complete with brass mounts and knobs, and wire-spring mattress, all for 20s; or with wool overlay, mattress, bolster and pillow for 30s, with no charge for packing.

Floor coverings varied according to the type of house being furnished and the room being considered. Many kitchens would have stone flagged floors and for other rooms the owner would purchase linoleum (sometimes referred to as lino) for the surrounds and only in the centre would there be a carpet, with perhaps a rug by the fireside. One significant advantage of the central carpet was that it could be turned round before wear became noticeable in any one area. Similarly the staircarpet was not fitted to the sides of the staircase but was a simple strip of carpet going down the centre of the stairs and held in place with brass rods; this again could be moved

to prevent wear on the edge of the steps. Underlay on the staircase was a series of pieces of felt where the feet trod. These items would all be purchased from the local furniture store.

The magazines of the period, and locally produced church magazines and town year books, all contained advertisements for household goods. Many people would buy their furniture and household goods from the same man that their parents had bought theirs from a generation earlier.

As we see the developments of the period, a span of over sixty years, we start to appreciate

how much life changed, and also what 'new-fangled things' were being introduced. Initially, a good source of clean, piped water was uncommon in most homes and of course the living room also served as the bathroom for that was where the tin bath would be placed in front of the fire on 'bath night'; other bodily washing generally took place at the kitchen sink, which frequently would have only a cold water tap, if it had a tap at all, hot water being boiled in a kettle or pan on the fire range. Therefore, we find in *The Illustrated London News* in 1897, Merryweathers'

advertising to supply water to mansions and estates. Having found it by use of divining rods, they would bore wells and install pumps and tanks, the tanks generally being placed on elevated ground some distance from the house. Other companies advertised that you could have 'water absolutely free from disease germs' by using the Berkefeld Filter as supplied to HRH The Prince of Wales, the House of Lords, and House of Commons. It also pointed out that a report by Joseph Lunt BSc FCS, British Institute of Preventive Medicine, says: 'Exhaustive experiments showed that with London tap-water strongly infected artificially WITH THE TYPHOID BACILLUS, not a single typhoid bacillus was detected IN THE FILTERED WATER for a period of 26 days.' Other offers included Maughan's Bath-Heaters, using their patent geyser – 'By this simple contrivance (incredible as it may appear) *cold* water is instantly changed to *hot* . . . by simply turning on water and gas, an immediate supply of hot or tepid water can be obtained; or a *Hot Bath* for child or adult can

be provided in case of sudden illness at any hour of day or night, without previous preparation or delay.'

Let us not forget that the lavatory, for many terraced homes, would be across the yard, perhaps next to the coal house, and indeed may have served more than one family; some had double seats, some even treble ones! A new toilet seat would be bought from the local joiner, who was probably also the undertaker. Toilet paper was not invented until the 1870s and frequently newspaper served this purpose, being torn or cut to suitable size and hung on a nail in the lavatory.

Today we turn a switch and have instant light – in early Victorian times they had oil lamps, candles or gas lighting. Light in bedrooms was a problem and 'night lights' were widely advertised. However there was a risk of them causing a fire and therefore those claiming to be of fire-proof nature had a strong selling point. In the latter part of the era electricity began to have some impact on the domestic scene, but it was only in the closing months of the Queen's reign that Ever-Ready torches and batteries were brought to this country from the United States.

Heating in rooms was generally by means of an open fire; iron fireplaces suitably coated in black lacquer, with tiled surrounds, are still found in the bedrooms of many Victorian houses. Alternatively, advertisements show heating stoves, burning coal or coke or mineral oil. Many of these could be ordered by post and would be delivered to the nearest station. For cooking, an iron 'black-leaded' fire range, complete with oven and sometimes a back boiler to heat water – thereby providing a hot-water system – would be installed in the kitchen, and

these would be purchased from local manufacturers or ironmongers.

In Victorian times walls would be coated with distemper in the poorer homes, whilst cellars would be 'whitewashed' with a mixture of lime, both preparations being purchased from the hardware store. Decorating could be hazardous, for many wallpapers were coloured with arsenical preparations and paints often contained deadly lead. *The Engineer,* in its issue of 1 November 1878, pointed out that white lead paint caused lead poisoning to be prevalent among both paint makers and painters. In the previous eleven years there had been 123 cases of illness related to carbonate of lead (common white paint) or arsenical or antimonial colouring matters in paint or on wallpapers. Firms were very quick to point out that *their* products contained no such dangers!

It would seem there was no shortage of wallpapers, or paper-hangings as they were called. In 1850 Cotterell Brothers of 500 Oxford Street were advertising 'the very superior character of their paper-hangings, selected with the utmost care from all the principal French and English manufacturers'. They claimed that a

stock of 30,000 to 50,000 pieces is always on hand 'so that they supply any quantity, of every grade, class and colour, for immediate use'. They also had establishments at Bath and Bristol. Further down Oxford Street, at Number 451, E T Archer 'Solicits an inspection of his superior paper-hangings (made by his patented inventions), fitted up on the walls of the very extensive range of Showrooms in panels, &c, &c, in every style of artistic arrangement, and for every kind of room.' The rooms were furnished with 'superior furniture' and also available were tapestries, carpets and best warranted floor-cloth, presumably linoleum.

Novelties in window curtaining in 1859 were 'Circassian [a thin worsted cloth] cloth curtains with rich silk borders, suitable for dining-room, drawing-room or library – the most effective article ever offered'.

It is only when you add ornaments, and perhaps a piano (or should I say a pianoforte) that a room is really furnished. J Tennant of 149 Strand could supply 'alabaster, marble, bronze, spar and other ornaments for the drawing room, library and dining room consisting of groups, figures, inkstands, candlesticks, obelisks, inlaid tables, paper weights, vases, &c.', whilst Mr Davis's manufactory at 20 Southampton Street, Covent Garden provided 'Pianofortes, self-playing Pianofortes and Organs, at Wholesale prices'. A self-playing Pianoforte with keys cost £45 whilst a six-octave cabinet cost £20; he could also offer 'a large Barrel Organ for a church which plays forty of the best psalm tunes'.

Something to Read

By the time Queen Victoria had come to the throne bookshops and circulating libraries had long been in evidence. Unlike today, they were places for socializing, more like select clubs, and booksellers often referred to themselves as 'The Trade'. However, compared to today, bookshops must have appeared dull with their poor lighting and the sombre covers, there being no brightly coloured jackets.

Many booksellers were also publishers; John Hatchard was one such. In 1797 he had taken over the premises of 173 Piccadilly, and had become publisher to the *Christian Observer* and also published *The Reports of the Society for Bettering the Conditions of the Poor*. In pre-Victorian days Hatchards was the meeting place for people such as William Wilberforce and E J Eliot who were members of this Society, which had as one of its main objectives the abolition of the slave trade. It was also at Hatchards that a meeting took place, in 1804, which led to the forming of the Horticultural Society, later to become the Royal Horticultural Society.

As early as 1814, John Hatchard had published a catalogue of books which ran to 7,000 items. Later, the firm moved to 187 Piccadilly and at one stage the family lived over the shop. John, in his latter years, 'from his long association with the Cloth', affected a semi-clerical attire himself. He was invariably dressed in black, his coat of the style of a bishop's frock coat, waistcoat buttoning to the throat wth an entirely plain front, and knee breeches and garters. Thomas, his second son, was a little more flighty in appearance with a blue dress coat with velvet collar, gilt buttons, white cravat, yellow waistcoat and brown nankeen trousers. When John Hatchard died in 1849 he was succeeded by Thomas, and after this by the founder's great-grandson, Henry Hudson, who took the business on until 1880.

Arthur Humphreys joined the company in 1881; his early days as a bookseller had been spent in the shop of William Mack of Bristol, a bookseller who is best remembered as the originator of the idea of 'Birthday Books',

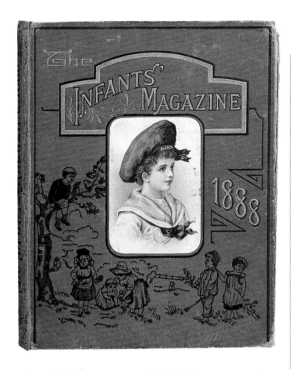

where blank spaces are left for the names of one's family and friends. He joined Hatchards as a young assistant and stayed with them for the next fifty years. He described for us the scene in those early days: 'The building at 187 Piccadilly where the business was conducted, was then one of the old residential houses, and in former days the Hatchard family lived in a large part of the front upper floors. At the back and on the lower floors, there were heaps of narrow staircases, dark corners and low-ceilinged attics all fitted with books. An atmosphere rather sombre and religious hung over the whole place. The assistants seemed to me to be all very old men either with beards or with side whiskers . . . Here in Piccadilly I saw the best of everything.' Fine carriages still brought people like Lord Shaftesbury, some still accompanied by powdered footmen in breeches and white stockings.

Hatchards often helped customers to develop their own private libraries, and Arthur Humphreys spent much of his time travelling the country, buying and selling collections of books. At a later date, the company was com-

missioned to be responsible for the private library of the Prince of Wales at Sandringham. When Edwin A M Shepherd bought Hatchards in 1891, and took Arthur Humphreys into partnership, the publishing side of the business had been sold off, but Humphreys started reprinting some of the old classics on handmade paper, calling the series 'The Royal Library'.

On the third floor a much enlarged second-hand book department was developed.

During the 1890s, famous clients included Rudyard Kipling and G K Chesterton and the firm also did much translating and printing of documents from other languages for Cecil Rhodes.

In the early years of the nineteenth century there were said to be over ninety booksellers in Edinburgh, which at that time had a population of about 130,000, although many people would be illiterate and very poor. John Menzies started in business in 1833, opening a rented shop at 61 Princes Street. He became an agent for Messrs Chapman & Hall, and this gave him the opportunity to sell all Charles Dickens's works in the east of Scotland; he also became agent for the new *Punch* magazine. Soon he was developing a wholesale trade and became known for finding almost any book, whether it be foreign, old or the latest published work.

John Menzies was a great innovator – initially *The Scotsman* newspaper was only available by subscription from the publisher, but he started selling it over the counter; from 1845 he issued regular monthly book lists; and he put staff on the Clyde steamers to serve the travellers. When the *Daily Mail* and the *Daily Express* were first published, the proprietors needed agents who would split up the large packages and distribute the papers to the small newsagents spread throughout the land; needless to say Menzies took on the task.

Of course, W H Smith was already in existence when Victoria came to the throne, but as a newspaper distributor. Each day newspapers were collected from Fleet Street by small carts and fast horses and then taken to coaching points for distribution across the country. The first person to have a railway bookstall is thought to be Horace Marshall, who opened one at Fenchurch Street station in London, but it was William Smith jnr. who really saw the potential of trade from travellers on the fast-developing railway system and opened the first railway bookstall at Euston in 1848. Soon the

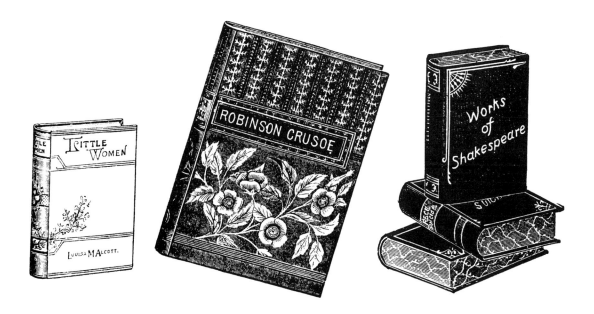

company had a network reaching up to the Scottish borders, with local stations acting as distribution points for nearby newsagents. It wasn't until early into the twentieth century that it started to develop shops away from the stations.

Looking at the mid-point of Victoria's reign, we can see something of the range of material that was available at that time. *Chambers's Journal* was already in its thirty-eighth year and was available monthly, price 7d. It contained articles on 'Tramways for the Suburbs', 'Comets', 'The Sublime Society of Beefsteaks', 'Poddins on the new Velocipede' and 'The Month: Science and Art'. This last item regularly told readers of new developments taking place, and today makes fascinating reading. *Blackwood's Magazine* for July 1869 featured articles on 'Recollections of Lord Byron', 'A New Theory of Earthquakes and Volcanoes', 'The Church Bill in the Lords' and 'Sketches in Polynesia – The Fijis', whilst *Macmillan's Journal*, also a monthly magazine, had articles which included one by Miss Octavia Hill on 'Organised Work among the Poor'. *Vanity Fair* was announcing that *The Graphic*, a new illustrated weekly newspaper was to be published

on 4 December 1869. The announcement drew attention to the increased growth of such journals 'in France, Germany, America, and even in the remote Australias'. It was a matter for surprise, that in England only one illustrated

compared with these narratives.'

Whilst reading may have become a more universal skill by the end of Queen Victoria's reign writing letters was a relaxation for young ladies who did not have access to the telephone as we do today. The paper and envelope makers, the stationers and those

newspaper of any pretensions should exist – presumably *The Illustrated London News*. *The Graphic* certainly lived up to the ideals propounded by the proprietors of providing 'Literary Excellence and Artistic Beauty'. It was published weekly, price 6d, 6½d by post.

Books of the period included: *Slang Dictionary*, published by John Camden Hotter of 74 and 75 Piccadilly, which contained 'Vulgar Words, Street Phrases, and Fast Expressions of High and Low Society; many with their etymology, and a few with their history traced'; *Debrett's Illustrated Peerage and Baronetage, with the Knightage for 1869*; a new edition of *The Water Babies* by Canon Kingsley; and *Tales of Old Travel* re-narrated by Henry Kingsley. The *Athenaeum* said of the last two: 'As for the sensational, most novels are tame

offering items for wedding presents certainly advertised widely in magazines of the period. In 1859 writing cases could be obtained from 2s 6d to 10s 6d whilst portable writing cases cost from 7s 6d; elegant pearl card cases cost from 2s 6d.

Wedding stationery was also advertised – enamelled envelopes stamped in silver with Arms, Crest or flowers were all readily available.

Dressing in Style

In early Victorian times wealthy families made half-yearly visits to London to purchase the latest fashionable goods from the developing range of high quality shops, such as Swan & Edgar, Heal & Son, Fortnum & Mason, Harvey Nichols and Clark & Debenham. These were all situated in the developing West End.

William Debenham realized the need to care for these wealthy families but also saw that middle-class families were becoming potentially valuable customers as their spending powers increased. Silks, furs and cashmeres, shawls, mantles and cloaks, lace and embroidery were still well displayed – they included laces from Brussels, Malines and Valenciennes and silks from France and Italy. However, he also made sure that machine-made linens and other less expensive items were available for the increasing numbers of customers who did not want such exclusive wares but nevertheless wished to be seen to belong to the upper strata of society, and on one occasion the firm purchased the whole stock of a Brussels glove manufacturer, selling them to its own customers and also to other retailers.

Debenhams was one of the first to introduce machine-knitted garments,

including the 'Jersey', an adaptation of the hand-knitted one-piece woollen trunk, with sleeves, knitted by the poor people of that island.

At that time Debenhams was probably unique in selling small quantities of cloth to dressmakers at wholesale prices, and also allowing them to take away samples of cloth to show to their clients. Such practices assured the firm of their trade, especially as it stocked the most fashionable goods of the best quality. In the 1890s an afternoon dress could require 15 yards of wide silk, 5 yards of skirt lining,

3 yards of horsehair cloth to stiffen the skirt, 4 yards of silk for a dust ruffle, various binds, beltings, and bonings, 4 cards of hooks and eyes, and 12 spools of thread, as well as 4 dozen fancy buttons!

Until the 1850s every seam of every dress, and of the numerous petticoats and other undergarments, had to be stitched by hand. Several people developed sewing machines, the first one in 1829 being created by a French tailor Barthelemy Thimmonier, but it was the machine which Isaac Merrit Singer patented in 1851 which revolutionized the production of clothing for all time. Singer opened shops to sell his machines, the first being in Glasgow in 1856, and by 1877 there were over one hundred and sixty. Indeed, it is suggested that he was the first manufacturer of any kind to develop a chain of retail shops specializing solely in its own product. A year before Singer patented his machine, the *World of Fashion* magazine had begun to include paper patterns 'in order that ladies of distinction and their dressmakers may possess the utmost facilities for constructing their costumes with the most approved Taste in the Highest and most Perfect Style of

Fashion'. The Butterick paper pattern, often referred to as the first, did not appear until the 1860s in America, and the 1870s in Britain. It was probably less complicated than those previous ones.

During the early years of the reign, and indeed later on, some of the larger London and provincial shops and stores sold clothes partly made, which were then completed by the customer's own dressmaker to obtain the desired fit. In some instances the skirt was completed and other material and trimmings were sold for the bodice of the dress. It is likely that Bainbridge of Newcastle in 1845 was one of the first to stock completely ready-made dresses – that year it advertised 'Sewed Muslin Dresses'. Later, in 1866, *The Illustrated London News* was advertising Jay's General Mourning House of Regent Street, in London; 'JAY'S PATENT EUTHEMIA, a self-expanding bodice, recommended to ladies in cases of sudden bereavement or any less painful emergency, when a ready-made and stylish dress is required at a moment's notice.' They had devised ways of coping with the varieties of women's figures without having to stock dresses in different measurements.

ALL THE DIFFERENCE!

*Haberdasher (to Assistant who has had the "swop"). "*WHY HAS THAT LADY GONE WITHOUT BUYING?"
*Assistant. "*WE HAVEN'T GOT WHAT SHE WANTS."
*Haberdasher. "*I'LL SOON LET YOU KNOW, MISS, THAT I KEEP YOU TO SELL WHAT I'VE GOT, AND NOT WHAT PEOPLE WANT!"

Spons' Household Manual of 1891, discussing 'How to Buy Clothes' states that 'Low-priced materials do not wear as well as those for which a fair-amount is paid; but it is not in the power of every woman to purchase materials which are necessarily expensive. The woman of small means will do well to confine her purchases to some well-established shop, famed rather for the soundness of its goods than for their apparent cheapness.' It went on: 'The greatest mistake is to be perpetually attempting to keep pace with "fashion". The best-dressed women are never "in the fashion", as it is represented in young ladies' journals. For economical dressing without dowdiness, the golden rule is to buy the best and soundest materials possible for your means, to keep to such quiet colours as will enable you to wear your dresses long without getting tired of them or tiring your friends; to buy a mantle, for instance, which is too good to need changing at the end of the year, but which is handsome enough to wear two seasons, and to bear retrimming or altering the third . . . many find it economical to have one good dress every year from a first-class dressmaker: this lasts and makes up again in many new forms, and serves as a model for making others less expensively . . . persons of moderate means should, as a rule, dress in black, or dark colours, as such are not conspicuous, and consequently do not tell their date as lighter articles do . . . it is safer to dress rather

BELOW, RIGHT, FACING PAGE, ABOVE: *A selection of models in fancy dress from the Liberty store. Ladies of fashion had their dressmaker copy the latest modes shown in the magazines and journals of the day.* FACING PAGE, BELOW: *Latest Paris fashions from* The Young Ladies Journal, *1871.*

older than younger than your age, it generally makes women past 30 look younger to dress thus; but much depends on the colours used.'

The same book gives details of how to choose 'Bathing and Swimming Dresses'. For instance: 'Where ladies bathe with gentlemen their dress must come below the knees, must have a skirt from the waist, and must have sleeves of some kind, and these, whether long or short, or however loose, are always uncomfortable for swimming, as they cling and impede the movements of the arm, whilst the whole dress is made heavier by these additions.' To avoid these problems it is suggested 'to make the drawers longer than is really needed, and to fasten them in at the knee'. However, shops such as Peter Robinson and the great Shawl & Cloak Emporium had been advertising these particular clothes since the 1860s.

Such books gave guidance to the traveller about what items of clothing were appropriate to a variety of situations, whether the person was dressing for visits to foreign lands, for a walking tour, for mourning, or for a journey on a yacht; in each case they gave details of shops specializing in such clothing.

From the classified advertisements in the journals of the period, we can see the various garments and choices of materials that were on offer. In *The Illustrated London News* in July 1859 the 'London and Paris Warehouse' of High Holborn was advertising that mauve was the fashionable colour and it had new mauve muslins at 7¾d a yard. French Flounced Bareges, a gauze-like silky dress fabric from Bareges in the French Pyrenees, was priced at 17s 6d for a full robe, and the 'Scarboro' Tweed Mantle was 12s 9d. At Jay's, end-of-the-season French silk dresses, 19 yards with flounces, 2½ guineas each! Still in London's West End, it was possible to buy new tartan spun silks and Spring Linsey Woolseys from Scott Adie's at 114 Regent Street, or Locke's Scotch silk cloaks in various shades and checks for summer wear from the Royal Clan Tartan Warehouse at 119 Regent Street.

For ladies' underwear, such as stays (stiff corsets) and petticoats, 'Ladies should visit WILLIAM CARTER's Wholesale and Retail Stay Establishment at 22 Ludgate Hill, St Pauls', where you were able to buy ladies' French

THE YOUNG LADIES JOURNAL, LATEST PARIS FASHIONS.

Nº 88. THE GOODS REPRESENTED IN THE ABOVE ILLUSTRATIONS CAN ALL BE PURCHASED FROM THE OLD-ESTABLISHED FIRM OF NICHOLSON & CO., 50, 51, AND 52 ST. PAUL'S CHURCHYARD, CORNER OF CHEAPSIDE, LONDON, AND OF WHOM PRICES MAY BE HAD UPON APPLICATION. May 1ˢᵗ 1871.

muslin or lace Jupons (a form of skirt) for which the costs ranged from 3s 9d to 21s, or ladies' crinoline watch-spring petticoats which ranged in price from 4s 9d to 25s. Ladies' elastic coutil (close woven canvas used in stay making) bodices sold at from 3s 11d to 10s 6d, whilst self-adjusting family and nursing stays cost 8s 6d to 25s; alternatively Carter and Houston in Regent Street offered 'The Self Adjusting Corset' at 12s 6d, and also had crinoline skirts and spring steel skirts at very low prices.

Petticoats to wear under the crinolines became popular in the early 1860s, especially as they could be seen as the crinoline was lifted up when the lady was getting into a carriage or going up stairs; there was a feeling of anticipation that more would come to view! Some were frilly muslin petticoats, others lace-trimmed, whilst others were made of warm flannel, many being made from material coloured by aniline dyes.

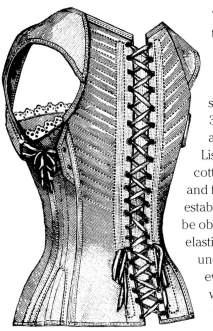

To complete the outfit Robertshaw's at 100 Oxford Street offered silk stockings at 3s 6d per pair, and Balbriggan, Lisle thread and cotton hosiery, and from the same establishment could be obtained 'patent elastic Merino underclothing of every degree of warmth'. The final touch came with the parasol and bonnet, for it was not desirable for young ladies to get sunburnt. W and J Sangster in Regent Street and Cheapside offered 'Every variety of SUN SHADES and PARASOLS, in Brocades, Glaces, Irish Lace, China Crape &c for fêtes or the promenade, from 7s 6d to 3 guineas each and upwards', and at Mrs Poland's showrooms in Crawford Street, off Portman Square, Tulle bonnets and white Braid bonnets, elegantly trimmed, cap complete, were available for 12s 6d.

While some were interested in fashion and style, others were more concerned about healthy living. One of those who experimented in producing clothing made entirely of animal hair, principally wool, was Dr Gustave Jaeger, professor of zoology and physiology at Stuttgart University. At first his creations were entirely underwear, 'Sanitary Woollen Underwear', avoiding the use of any vegetable fibres such as linen or cotton. Later his ideas were translated into a full way of living and even Ambrose Heal made woollen mattresses to sell in his shop.

Lewis Tomalin, an accountant, came across Dr Jaeger's book, *Health Culture*, in 1880 and was so enthralled by his ideas that he made a bonfire of the family linen, underwear and

sheets and replaced them with ones of fine woollen taffeta. In 1884 he opened a shop in Fore Street, in London, not to make a livelihood, but to share this enthusiasm with others. Advertisements claimed that Jaeger's knitted woollen suits for boys, supplied in either natural brown or indigo-dyed wool, with their closely fitted shape were tasteful, cheap and very durable; he claimed that their shape was the 'guarantee for the sanitary perfection of this outer clothing'. Patented knitted sleeping garments were sold, which could be supplied fitted with a hood for those who were bald or had thinning hair, and there were sanitary woollen petticoats and aprons for women and children. Soon Tomalin's philanthropic venture was growing into an economically sound business and within a short period of time he opened further shops; by 1900 there were twenty. It was about this time that Jaeger first introduced camel hair into Britain. It wasn't until the 1930s that Jaeger shops abandoned their 'health' principles and concentrated on good fashion.

Beauty is in the Eye of the Beholder

When clothing is not changed very frequently and the opportunities to bath are rather rare then people do not make good company, unless other measures are taken. 'Viner's Rose Geranium and Verbena Extracts' claimed pre-eminence for combining the peculiar properties of these favourite exotics. The two extracts, unique perfumes, were recommended for the handkerchief, where their refreshing qualities were of benefit 'in all crowded assemblies' – so reads Viner's advertisement in *The Illustrated London News* of 1844. The extracts were available from its depot in Maddox Street, and at the principal houses.

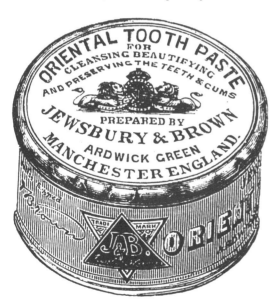

J & E Atkinson, who were perfumers in Old Bond Street in 1844, were similarly respectfully informing the public that they had received their stock of new perfumes from the South of France, and that they were finer than they had been for many years. Their stock consisted of 'Essences, Pomades, Powders, etc and in all the variety, distinguishing the flower gardens of Nice, Grass, Montpelier'.

Jermyn Street, not far from Piccadilly, was a rival to Bond Street as a shopping centre. It was the exclusive address of many London bachelors of 'substance', and many famous men have lived or lodged in the street, including the poet Thomas Gray; William Pitt;

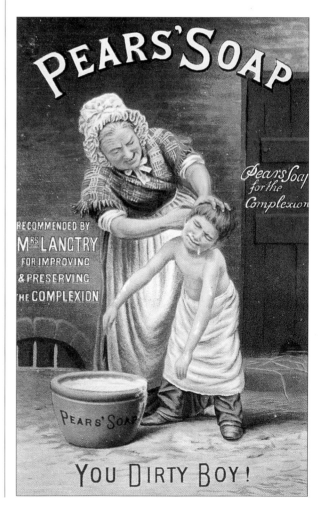

OBSERVE!
••••••••••••••••
I AM

The Spirit of Health,

and my message is to the Wise.
I crown, with a fadeless wreath,
those who obey my laws and avail
themselves of my counsels. The
flowers that I give do not wither,
and the fragrance of my roses is
perpetual. I bring bloom to the
cheek—strength to the body—joy
to the heart. The talisman with
which I work never fails. Vast
numbers have felt its
power, and testified to
its virtues. It is

BEECHAM'S PILLS,
THE WORLD'S MEDICINE!

A perfect remedy for disorders of the
liver, stomach, and digestive organs,
accompanied by nervous debility.

If you are in any degree a sufferer, let the
SPIRIT OF HEALTH inspire you to try

BEECHAM'S PILLS.
THEY ARE
WORTH A GUINEA A BOX.

children solely on the manufacture of bone toothbrushes, which were only warranted if 'FLORIS Jermyn Street' was inscribed on the handle. Indeed 'if it happens, which is very rare, that some hairs become loose, they not only change them, but are obliged to the purchaser for the information'. They were 'sold in a variety of patterns, at 1s set in bone, or 2s set in ivory'. The former Miss Mary Ann Floris married Mr J R D Bodenham and they continued the family ownership from about 1870, a link continued to the present day by members of the Bodenham family.

In the days when many illnesses, such as smallpox, caused damage to the complexion, to have a clear skin free from blemish must have been a joy. According to an advertisement,

Sir Thomas Lawrence, the fashionable painter; Sir Walter Scott; and Admiral Lord Nelson, who occupied 'chambers' above the Floris shop at Number 89. It was here that Juan Faminias Floris, who had come from the island of Minorca, had set up his perfumery in 1730.

By 1800, the firm is referred to as 'Comb Makers to HRH The Prince of Wales'. Exquisite tortoiseshell and ivory combs had become fashionable among the clientele: some were hand-carved and had come from Spain, some were accessories for the hair. Natural sponges and bone toothbrushes were also in demand and from the 1870s were served from the superb Spanish Mahogany shop-fittings (which are still in use today) which came from the Great Exhibition. Around this period the firm employed a married couple and their three

Once Beauty bore a sunshade large
To shield her soft white skin,
And o'er her charming
features fair
An envious veil did pin.

But now in old Sol's burning rays
She dares to sweetly slumber,
For BEETHAM puts her all
to rights
with GLYC'RINE & CUCUMBER.

if you used Sulpholine Lotion every night for a week, 'this peculiar, agreeable fluid' has the 'faculty of always producing a clear smooth skin by restoring its healthy action'. It was sold by chemists everywhere at 9d a bottle.

Rimmel, Perfumers of 96 Strand, 24 Cornhill and Crystal Palace was advertising in 1859 two 'sorts' of 'Lotion for the Skin. No.1 Beautifies and preserves the complexion, No.2 removes pimples, tan, freckles, and sunburns', and they were available from all perfumers and chemists, priced 2s 9d, 4s 6d and 8s 6d.

Messrs John Gosnell & Co held the trade mark 'Cherry Blossom' in 1887, but made perfume, toilet powder and soap – and using a full-page picture of a nun in the Jubilee Celebration number of *The Graphic*, advertised

'Nun Nicer'! Other preparations to cure skin problems were numerous and we must remember that a pale, unblemished skin, rather than a sun-tanned complexion was favoured, as the latter was a sign that the person worked out of doors, a lower class of person! Rowland's Kalydor, 'Patronised and Sanctioned by her Majesty the QUEEN, the Royal Family, and several Courts of Europe' claimed to 'effectually eradicate all Pimples, Spots, Blotches, Redness, Tan, Freckles, and other defects of the Skin. The Radiant Bloom it imparts to the Cheek, and the softness and delicacy it induces on the hands, arms and neck, render it indispensable to every toilet.' This remedy, which was available at all chemists and perfumers, was also a safeguard against chilblains and chapped skin.

The same company, was advertising, again in *The Illustrated London News*, in 1844, that its 'Rowland's Odonto', or 'Pearl Dentifrice', which was 'compounded of the rarest and most fragrant exotics', eradicated tartar and spots of incipient decay from the teeth, and 'imparts a pearl-like whiteness, and fixes them firmly in the Gums. It strengthens, braces and renders the gums of a healthy red, and bestows a grateful sweetness and perfume to the breath.' So, no doubt, if one used Viner's Rose Geranium and Verbena Extracts and Rowland's Odonto, you would be free of body odour and bad breath, and be good to live with!

An article in 1879 in *The Illustrated London News* warns of 'Dangerous Soaps', saying that

He also developed a gentle soap suitable for tender skins, one which was delicately perfumed with the flowers of an English garden, and was also transparent. Soon other manufacturers tried to copy it, making cheap alternatives in similar wrappings and so, to protect his reputation, he announced that he would sign each packet with 'my own quill' thus exposing 'those fraudulent practices'.

In 1835 he brought his grandson, Francis, into the business and the company became known as A & F Pears, but it was not until 1862 that it was decided to expand the business. Francis Pears' eldest daughter, Mary, married Thomas J Barratt and he also became her partner. Thomas Barratt was very skilful in marketing and advertising and it was he who made their soaps known throughout the world.

He worked on the basis that Pears Soap was safe and healthy, and that it made its users more beautiful. He was one of the first people to use 'glamour advertising', making Mrs Lily Langtry his first star when she said: 'Since using Pears Soap, I have discarded all others,' and 'I prefer it to any other soap.' *Punch* magazine made fun of this testimonial by getting Harry Furniss to draw a cartoon showing a tramp laboriously writing his testimonial to Pears: 'Two years ago I used your soap, since

at 'a recent sitting of the Academy of Medicine Dr Revell read a paper on the necessity of preventing perfumers from selling poisonous or dangerous soaps'. It was followed by a note on 'The Infant's Bath', going on to state: 'Children are great sufferers from the effects of bad soap. Pears Transparent Soap is absolutely pure, while it is fragrant.' Although not obvious at the beginning, both items are advertisements for Pears Soap for the piece ends: 'Pears Transparent Soap, of Chemists and Perfumers everywhere. Wholesale and Retail of A & F Pears 91 Great Russell Street, London.'

Andrew Pears left Mevagissy in 1789, having completed his apprenticeship as a hairdresser, and established himself as a hairdresser in Gerrard Street, in Soho. It was a fashionable, residential part of London and with his skills he soon attracted a distinguished clientele whom he visited in their own homes. In his shop he manufactured beauty aids such as rouge, creams, powders and dentifrice.

He won't be happy till he gets it!

then I have used no other.' However Barratt used this to the company's benefit.

Another of Barratt's schemes took place in 1880. It was at a time when many French 10-centime pieces were in circulation in England, and were accepted as the equivalent of English pennies. Barratt imported about a quarter-of-a-million of them and defaced them by stamping the name Pears on each one. Then he put them into circulation. There was no law forbidding such action, but it did lead to an Act of Parliament which declared all foreign coins to be illegal tender. Pears coins were then withdrawn.

The adjacent illustrations are examples of some of his famous advertisements; another is the one using the portrait known as 'Bubbles', by Sir John Everett Millais, President of the Royal Academy – a painting of his grandson watching a soap bubble he had just blown through a clay pipe. It was exhibited at the Royal Academy, then sold to *The Illustrated London News* for use as a presentation plate in its magazine, before being sold to Pears for £2,200 for use as an advertisement.

Another innovative idea, which helped to promote Pears' products, was *The Pears Shilling Cyclopaedia*, which was first published in 1897 by A & F Pears. All 600,000 copies of the first edition were sold and a further edition had to be printed. It combined everyday practical information with general knowledge in an inexpensive volume, at a time when the larger dictionaries and encyclopaedias were beyond the reach of ordinary people.

A & F Pears were appointed Royal Warrant Holders by Queen Victoria and at the Paris Exhibi-

tion in 1900 gained the Grand Prix, the only one ever awarded solely for toilet soap.

Novelties need advertising! It has always been so and so it was in 1859.

In the classified advertisements in *The Illustrated London News* on 9 July there appeared: 'RIMMEL'S BOUQUET is the PERFUME of the SEASON – Sweet as a May morning; pure and white as crystal' – of course, it was available from perfumers and chemists – and 'FORGET ME NOT, an entirely new and exquisite perfume, distilled from the sweetest flowers by L T PIVER, Perfumer and Glover.' Then, as now, counterfeiting of such items was a problem and therefore the manufacturers included in their advertisement 'To avoid all counterfeits, each bottle will bear a gilt stamp, and be wrapped up in a pretty fancy box, price 3s 6d.' This perfume was available from Pivers at 160 Regent Street, but also from a number of other suppliers which included Dent, Allcroft and Co of 97 Wood Street, better known to us today as 'Dents', the long-established glove manufacturers, originally based in Worcester.

He's got it ! – He's happy now.

The Tragedy of Death
– An Ever Living Trade

Death has always been a time of grieving, but the outward expression of that grief has had different effects on trade through the generations. In Victorian times mourning probably reached its peak and many establishments catered solely for the supply of clothing for what was often an extended period of time.

The custom of wearing black has come to us from the time of the restoration of the

J. MIDWOOD & Co.,

Joiners and Undertakers

Beaumont Street, Northgate,

HUDDERSFIELD.

FUNERALS COMPLETELY FURNISHED.

All kinds of Jobbing Work

Executed on the SHORTEST NOTICE.

Mourning, at the most advantageous prices . . . and in consequence of the demise of Her Majesty he has determined to sell off the whole of his present very valuable stock of white and coloured dresses . . .'. All advertisers at that time assured their customers that they would make no commercial gain out of the nation's grief.

The period of mourning varied according to circumstances. When the Queen of Hanover, Queen Victoria's aunt, died in 1841, court mourning was only twenty-one days, and after the first two weeks ladies could once again use coloured ribbons and fans with their black

monarchy in 1660. In 1821, following the death of Queen Caroline Amelia Elizabeth, J Millard, who had the East India Warehouses in London's Cheapside, 'most respectfully informs his friends and the Nobility he has to offer to their notice an excellent assortment of Family

FACING PAGE: *Jay's Mourning Warehouse stocked every item required by gentlemen and ladies of fashion in their bereavement.*
RIGHT: *Peter Robinson of Regent Street also specialized in supplying mourning wear at very short notice and with the services of a dressmaker!*

FASHIONS FOR 1887.

On receipt of Letter or Telegram, Mourning Goods will be forwarded to any part of England on approbation, no matter the distance, with an EXCELLENT FITTING DRESSMAKER (if desired), without any extra charge whatever.   Address—

PETER ROBINSON,

MOURNING WAREHOUSE, REGENT-ST.

BLACK MATERIALS
BY THE YARD
AND THE NEW MAKES OF
BLACK SILKS
ARE
MARVELLOUSLY CHEAP,
AND STRONGLY RECOMMENDED
FOR GOOD WEAR.
PATTERNS FREE.

MATERIAL COSTUMES,
SILK COSTUMES.
ENTIRELY NEW DESIGNS IN GREAT VARIETY,
AND VERY MODERATE IN PRICE.

PETER ROBINSON,
THE COURT AND GENERAL MOURNING
WAREHOUSE,
256 to 262, REGENT-STREET.

PETER ROBINSON { MOURNING WAREHOUSE,
REGENT-STREET, LONDON.

silks and velvets. However, family mourning was longer than Court or national mourning and could last for up to two years, especially for a widow mourning her late husband. Even children had to wear black outfits for several months; at the very least they would have black-edged handkerchiefs. Special black-edged writing paper was also bought for use with black-edged envelopes which were sealed with black wax.

Sometimes the supply of mourning outfits and the undertaking service were conducted from the same premises. Advertising of such services was prevalent in all the magazines of the period. Peter Robinson's of Regent Street advertised regularly in the classified columns, and although the company sold many general lines it devoted much space to its 'Court and Family Mourning Warehouse'. It claimed 'that on receipt of a letter or telegram mourning goods will be forwarded to any part of England on approbation – no matter the distance – with

MOURNING FOR FAMILIES.

JAY'S
experienced
DRESSMAKERS
and
MILLINERS
Travel to any part of the Kingdom, Free of expense to purchasers.
They take with them Dresses and Millinery, besides Patterns of Materials, at 1s. per yard and upwards, all marked in plain figures, and at same price as if purchased at the Warehouse, in Regent-street.
Reasonab e estimates are also given for Household Mourning. at a great saving to large or small families.
Funerals at stated charges conducted in London or Country.

JAY'S,
The London General Mourning Warehouse,
REGENT-STREET, W.

CHANTILLY LACE COSTUME,
ON SATIN FOUNDATION WITH JETTED PANEL,
Including Lace and Trimming for Bodice,
5½ Guineas.

NOVELTIES

AT

JAY'S.

ELEGANT TEA GOWN.
BLACK, OR BLACK AND WHITE CHINA SILK.
5½ Guineas.

FACING PAGE: *Fashion need not be sacrificed to grief at Jay's.*

RIGHT: *This cartoon from* Punch *in the mid-1880s, satirizes the etiquette by which society now measured degrees of mourning.*

TRUE FEMININE DELICACY OF FEELING.

Emily (who has called to take Lizzie to the great Murder Trial). "WHAT DEEP BLACK, DEAREST!"

Lizzie. "YES. I THOUGHT IT WOULD BE ONLY DECENT, AS THE POOR WRETCH IS SURE TO BE FOUND GUILTY."

Emily. "AH! I HEARD IT WAS EVEN BETTING WHICH WAY THE VERDICT WOULD GO, SO I ONLY PUT ON *Half* MOURNING!"

an excellent fitting Dressmaker (if desired) without any extra charge whatever'. Its mourning establishment became unofficially known as 'Black Peter Robinson's'.

Also in Regent Street was Jay's Mourning Warehouse, which was established in 1841. It sometimes took a full page in magazines such as *The Graphic*, advertising as Maison Jay's. The premises occupied three adjoining houses.

On the frontage was a large sign proclaiming 'The London General Mourning Warehouse', and above the sign was evidence of the Royal Appointments held by the firm. A writer of the period describes the interior for us: how, after ascending a long flight of stairs, you emerge into a softly carpeted, large lofty room; there was a quietness, an harmonious hush about the whole place – it had a 'total unshoppy character'. At either side of the doorway were large mahogany tables where you could sit and call for any mourning items you required. In the showrooms were large sofas, easy chairs and dazzling mirrors and 'a bevy of bright eyed fair damsels, clad in black silk, who will lay before us every description of mourning we may require. Mantles all a-bristle with bugles and beads, widow's caps as light as a feather and trimmed with long streamers like fairies' wings, and bonnets of the most subtle design. For those wishing to buy a cloak the young damsels would immediately put it on to show the fit, whilst in the silk department there would be silks and satins in delicate shades of slate-colour, grey, mauve and purple and delicate robes of palest violet tint fairly frosted with crystal spots.' The commentator concludes that our ashes must be properly selected, our sackcloth must be of the finest quality, and our grief goes for nothing if not fashionable!

When the Nicholson brothers opened the Argyll General Mourning & Mantle Warehouse in 1854 they also chose Regent Street. They advertised in the Death column of the *Morning Post*, 'respectfully begging to intimate to ladies whose bereavements demand the immediate adoption of mourning attire, that every requisite for a complete outfit of mourning can be supplied at a moment's notice, and that many unpleasant occurrences arising from delay on melancholy occasions are thereby obviated'. The point 'at a moment's notice' referred to etiquette decreeing that widows and daughters must not be seen out of doors before the funeral!

Nicholsons also issued a book called *Mourning Etiquette* which they supplied free of charge so that 'all trouble may be avoided in deciding the degree of mourning proper to be worn under various losses'.

ABOVE AND FACING PAGE: *Ladies could be fully fitted in their mourning clothes without leaving home before the funeral, as indeed etiquette dictated, with Jay's service 'at a moment's notice'.*

The Well-Dressed Man

'It is a very foolish thing for a man not to be Well-dressed, according to his rank and way of life,' wrote Lord Chesterfield, and shopkeepers and manufacturers of the day made sure men did not forget it. The gentlemen's outfitter was the hosier, hatter, glover and shirtmaker, as well as being the tailor.

In London, Burlington Arcade was one of the homes of gentlemen's fashion. When it was built in 1818 it was the first shopping arcade in England and from an early date was regarded as a place of taste and architectural skill, 'the shops being appropriately fitted for the sale of books, prints, jewellery . . . and other articles of fashionable demand'. Unfortunately the arcade was badly damaged by a fire in 1836,

but rose again to its former glory. Lord's hosiers and glovers has been part of the arcade from its earliest days. Other areas with particular masculine connections are Jermyn Street and Savile Row.

In Victorian times men rarely went out without a hat. It was possible to distinguish a person's social standing by the hat he was wearing; for instance, rich men would wear black silk top hats, tradesmen ones appropriate to their task, especially those who carried loads on their heads.

Lock & Co have been hatters in the same premises in St James's Street since the middle

LEFT: *This man is evidently aspiring to the status conferred by the tall silk hat in the window.*
FACING PAGE, ABOVE: *Tradesman were not above trading on the vanity of their customers' aspirations.*
BELOW: *At the other end of the market, ready-made tailoring was becoming more accessible.*

Temptation.

FASHIONS FOR 1845.

"A PIN FOR YOUR SCARF, SIR? HERE'S AN ARTICLE WE HAVE SOLD A GREAT MANY OF."

opened an outfitters in Basingstoke in 1856. He came from a farming background and had seen the smocks worn by the shepherds and farmers; he realized that they were warm in winter but cool in summer, were easy to wear and also kept the wearer moderately dry. With the help of a local cotton mill owner he developed a similar cloth which was proofed in the yarn before weaving, without the use of rubber, and then woven closely and proofed again in the piece – he called his cloth Gabardine, a word of French extraction. The material was completely waterproof, cool and comfortable to wear, and as it did not tear it proved ideal for field sports and for fishing.

of the eighteenth century. In 1850 Lock's received instructions from a William Coke of Norfolk, to make him a specially hardened round felt hat to protect his game-keepers' heads. James Lock developed the specification and then got Thomas and William Bowler of Southwark to manufacture it for him, hence the name 'Bowler Hat', or sometimes 'Coke Hat'.

Genuine Panama hats are woven in Panama, but the black band sometimes worn around the hat was instituted for the mourning period for Queen Victoria.

Thomas Burberry, then only twenty-one,

Unlike rubber-based waterproof clothes his garments could 'breathe'. Shop-keepers like Burberry would take advantage of the local seasonal markets and fairs, such as the 'Michaelmas Fair' held in October when farm workers, carters and cowmen would come to be hired by the local farmers, and shops advertised Michaelmas clothing and other special offers.

Later, in 1889 when Thomas Burberry wanted to get a part of the London trade he arranged for his younger son, Arthur, to go to the Jermyn Street Hotel to meet potential customers, to take their orders and give them fittings. By the close of the century Burberrys had taken premises in the Haymarket and developed a warehouse and wholesale premises in Golden Square.

Back in Basingstoke, in 1905, a major fire completely destroyed the premises, and the reports give us a picture of what the store must have been like towards the end of the nineteenth century. The fire had started at 6pm when an assistant in the millinery department was lighting up the front window. A piece of material fell on to the taper she was carrying and burst into flames. Within seconds the fire had spread to curtains on display in the next window and before the fire brigade could arrive the shop was an inferno. At that time Burberrys employed twenty-seven dress-makers in a workshop in the rear

FUR COATS
FOR GENTLEMEN.
A GOOD FUR-LINED OVER-COAT FOR £10.

"HANDSOME FURS.— The International Fur Store, 163, Regent Street, London, of which Mr. T. S. Jay is manager, have now ready one of the choicest stocks of fine Furs in the world, and from their special facilities are enabled to offer extra inducements to persons desiring these garments. The goods now made up are in new and beautiful designs, and consist of sealskin jackets, coats, and dolmans of selected skins, the perfection of colour, and all of artistic finish. THEIR FUR-LINED COATS FOR GENTLEMEN ARE NOT EQUALLED IN THE WORLD. In addition they manufacture fur gloves for ladies and gentlemen, fur capes, and fur boas—in fact, every garment in the fur line."—*New York Spirit of the Times.*

Only Address,
163, REGENT STREET, LONDON

of the premises; twenty-five lived above the shop and a further twenty slept in a house on the other side of the road.

Standards of personal hygiene, particularly with regard to changing one's clothing, were not what we expect today, but of course they

did not have easy-wash fabrics nor did they have automatic washing machines and modern detergent. It was quite expected that a man would wear the same shirt on several consecutive days, and in the case of the labourer, perhaps also sleep in it as well. Shirts were advertised which had reversible cuffs, thereby enabling the wearer to give the impression of having a clean shirt while in fact only having clean cuffs. Other companies were advertising that they would remake your old

BELOW: *The forerunner of the Gentleman's complete outfitter. Shops such as this were tailors, shirtmakers, hatters, glovers and hosiers.*

"DE GUSTIBUS," &c., &c.

Snip. "THAT'S A SWEET THING FOR A WAISTCOAT, SIR, AND WOULD LOOK UNCOMMON WELL UPON YOU, SIR."

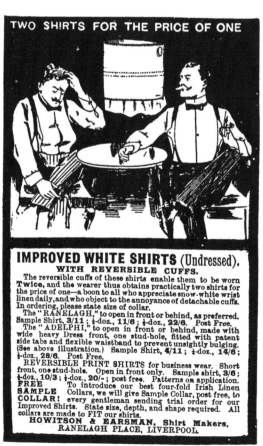

TWO SHIRTS FOR THE PRICE OF ONE

IMPROVED WHITE SHIRTS (Undressed).
WITH REVERSIBLE CUFFS.

The reversible cuffs of these shirts enable them to be worn **Twice**, and the wearer thus obtains practically two shirts for the price of one—a boon to all who appreciate snow-white linen daily, and who object to the annoyance of detachable cuffs. In ordering, please state size of collar.
The "RANELAGH," to open in front or behind, as preferred. Sample Shirt, 3/11 ; ½-doz., 11/6 ; ¼-doz., 22/6. Post Free.
The "ADELPHI," to open in front or behind, made with wide heavy Dress front, one stud-hole, fitted with patent side tabs and flexible waistband to prevent unsightly bulging. (See above illustration.) Sample Shirt, 4/11 ; ½-doz., 14/6 ; ¼-doz., 28/6. Post Free.
REVERSIBLE PRINT SHIRTS for business wear. Short front, one stud-hole. Open in front only. Sample shirt, 3/6 ; ¼-doz., 10/3 ; ¼-doz., 20/- ; post free. Patterns on application.
FREE To introduce our best four-fold Irish Linen **SAMPLE** Collars, we will give Sample Collar, post free, to **COLLAR!** every gentleman sending trial order for our Improved Shirts. State size, depth, and shape required. All collars are made to FIT our shirts.
HOWITSON & EARSMAN, Shirt Makers,
RANELAGH PLACE, LIVERPOOL.

SMART IN APPEARANCE

and Up-to-Date in Style is the opinion of all who have seen Hanna and Co.'s Pure Irish Linen Collars, Cuffs, and Shirts. You are invited to write for Samples and Illustrated Price List, which will be sent Post Free, and judge for yourself.

Shirts from 27s. 6d. half dozen, post free. Old Shirts made equal to new, with Best Linen Neck - Bands, Fronts, and Cuffs, 14s. per half dozen.

Four-fold Collars, 5s. per dozen ; Cuffs, from 6s. 11d. per dozen. Ladies' Collars, 4-fold, from 3s. 6d. per dozen ; Cuffs, from 7s. 6d. per dozen. Dozens post free.

Hanna and Co.'s High-Class Irish Linens are equal to the Famous Irish Linens of 50 years ago. Being Hand-Woven and Grass Bleached, give Endless Wear, and retain their Beautiful Snow-White Appearance.

Irish Damask Table-Linen. Irish Cambric Handkerchiefs. (Dozens post free). Ladies' Irish Underclothing. All supplied at Lowest Wholesale Prices.

NOTE.—CARRIAGE IS PAID ON ALL ORDERS OF £1 and upwards within the United Kingdom.

Write at once for Samples and Illustrated Price List post free. Address Dept. D,

HANNA & CO., 4. BEDFORD ST., BELFAST
(Factory : LURGAN, the Home of the Linen Hand-Loom Industry.)

shirts equal to new, with best linen neck bands, fronts and cuffs. Hann & Co's shirts were made of hand-woven, grass bleached Irish linen which would give endless wear and retain their beautiful snow-white appearance. However for the poorer men linen was too expensive and their shirts were mainly made of bleached or coloured cotton.

Over their shirts men often wore waist-coats, a morning coat and, if going out, a great coat as well. Towards the end of Victoria's reign younger men wore smart waistcoats and jack-ets in much brighter colours, although some of the satin waistcoats from the 1850s were also very colourful.

For less formal suits, for riding and other country pursuits, worsted and tweed would

be used. Many of the woollen worsted materials came from the mills of the Pennine towns of Yorkshire whilst some of the tweeds came from the Cotswolds and the West Country. Egerton Burnett held twenty-one royal appointments for its serges, made in Somerset, whilst Henry Pese & Co in Darlington advertised cross warp serges, at loom prices, which had been dyed by a special process 'for seaside, tourist and travelling wear. Guaranteed to withstand sun, rain and sea water.'

Not many people could afford to dress in style in Victorian times, and even those of the upper classes sometimes resorted to loaning or hiring clothes for special occasions. Advertisements appeared in national journals for 'Left-off clothes, uniforms and miscellaneous property, &c', all claiming the highest price given! Monmouth Street, not far from Covent Garden, in London, became known as 'Rag Fair' because of the large numbers of shops which sold secondhand clothes, boots and shoes. The shoes were generally kept in cellar shops, with access from the pavement down a flight of steps. It is said that many of the goods sold in such shops were stolen, either in burglaries, or by servants, workers or shop-lifters taking clothing and then using it to raise cash. Even some young men coming to the City to start their careers would use such shops to purchase their first suit. Lower down the scale,

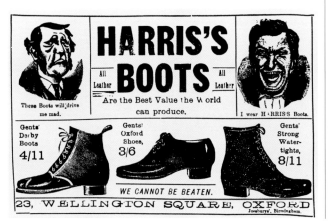

Garden, where he sold men's second-hand clothing and the occasional suit that some tailor had made and which did not fit the customer.

In those early days this sort of business was the 'norm', but as the years passed the firm started buying military clothing, often left following the decease of an officer and brought into the shop by his widow.

In 1881 the business moved to a double-fronted shop, 20–21 King Street, which he leased, allowing his sons to run the business on the ground floor whilst upstairs, semi-retired, he cleaned and arranged the stock. Old man Moses died in 1894 and it was

stall holders bought old clothing, cut out the best pieces of material and sold these to jobbing tailors, who would use them as patches.

It was in such surroundings that Moses Moses grew up. He spent his early days in the slums around King's Cross and Euston railway stations, but probably started business as a second-hand clothes dealer in the 1850s. This was, however, no ordinary Jew who started in this way. Moses Moses was a scholar and a lay reader in the synagogue. In 1860 he leased two small shops in Covent

only after this that the shop took on the name with which we are now familiar – Moss Bros.

The Chemist's Shop

The Victorian era was the age of medicines prepared by the individual pharmacist, often to meet a specific set of local circumstances, such as the climate or the type of industry of the area. The Pharmaceutical Society of Great Britain was formed in 1841 and in 1852 a register of chemists and druggists was started. However it was ordinary chemists and druggists who continued to be the main suppliers of medicines and related items to the public.

In the Lancashire port of Fleetwood James Lofthouse set up as a pharmacist and chemist in 1865. Many of his customers were fishermen going out to the north Atlantic fishing grounds where they would experience some very harsh weather conditions. No doubt the fogs and frosts and bitter winds played havoc with their chests and bronchial tubes and they sought James's help on their return. He made it his task to discover the best formula of liquorice, capsicum, eucalyptus and menthol to give them respite and comfort – today we know his preparation as Fisherman's Friend.

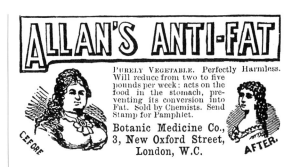

Many men like him would work in that way over a hundred years ago. Across on Yorkshire's east coast T J Smith similarly looked after the needs of the community in Hull. There the main industry was also fishing and a by-product was cod-liver oil, a very different product from the one we know today. In those Victorian days

ABOVE: *'Before' and 'after' may be exaggerated in this advertisement!*
RIGHT: *A nineteenth-century Boot's store.*

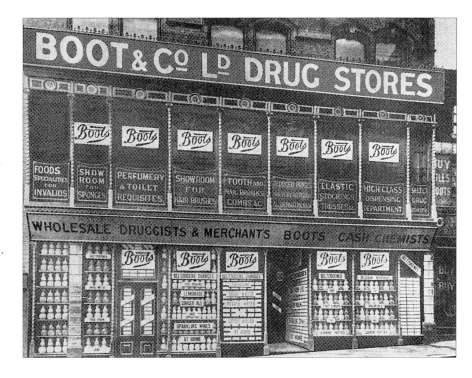

A WONDERFUL MEDICINE

BEECHAM'S PILLS

Are universally admitted to be worth a Guinea a Box for Bilious and Nervous Disorders such as Wind and Pain in the Stomach, Sick Headache, Giddiness, Fullness and Swelling after Meals, Dizziness and Drowsiness, Cold Chills, Flushings of Heat, Loss of Appetite, Shortness of Breath, Costiveness, Scurvy, Blotches on the Skin, Disturbed Sleep, Frightful Dreams and all Nervous and Trembling Sensations, &c. The first dose will give relief in twenty minutes. This is no fiction, for they have done so in countless cases. Every sufferer is earnestly invited to try one Box of these Pills, and they will be acknowledged to be

WORTH A GUINEA A BOX

For Females of all ages these Pills are invaluable. No Female should be without them. There is no medicine to be found to equal BEECHAM'S PILLS for removing any obstruction or irregularity of the system. If taken according to the directions given with each Box, they will soon restore females of all ages to sound and robust health. This has been proved by thousands who have tried them, and found the benefits which are ensured by their use.

For a weak stomach, impaired digestion, and all disorders of the liver, they act like magic and a few doses will be found to work wonders upon the most important organs of the human machine. They strengthen the whole muscular system, restore the long lost complexion, bring back the keen edge of appetite, and arouse into action, with the rosebud of health, the whole physical energy of the human frame. These are facts testified continually by members of all classes of society, and one of the best guarantees to the nervous and debilitated is BEECHAM'S PILLS have the largest sale of any Patent Medicine in the world.

Full directions are given with each Box. Prepared by

THOMAS BEECHAM, St. Helen's, Lancashire, England

And Sold by all Chemists and Patent Medicine Dealers everywhere.

In Boxes, at 1s. 1½d. and 2s. 9d. each.

LEFT: *Another famous name, Beechams, were selling their celebrated pills in chemist's shops across the land.*
BELOW: *Chemist's shop windows were easily recognizable by the large coloured-glass flasks and bottles on display.*
FACING PAGE: *A Boot's 'own brand' version of a popular remedy.*

it was dark brown in colour with a strong fishy flavour, but nevertheless in 1883 he won a gold medal for the quality of his oil, for already he was working hard to refine and blend it and make it more palatable. Another small part of his business was selling bandages and wound dressings, but it would be several years after the end of the Victorian period that the firm, T J Smith & Nephew became widely known for products such as Elastoplast.

Today, in small towns, and in many museums, it is possible to see chemist's shops which appear to have changed little from Victorian times. In the window are still the large glass bottles of coloured liquids, and behind the counter the rows of little drawers, each one bearing the name of some drug or herb. Above these would be shelf upon shelf of bottles, again each one having upon it the name of the preparation in an abbreviated Latin form. Poisons were often stored in dark green bottles which sometimes had fluted sides to make them even more distinguishable. Salt-glazed stoneware or earthenware jars were used to store creams

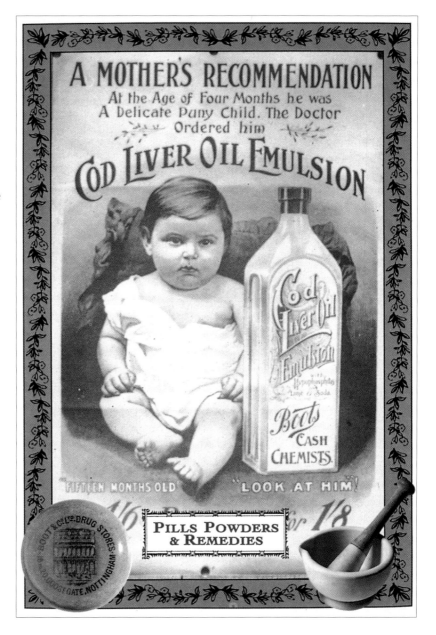

and ointments and similar ones were also used to contain live medicinal leeches, which were commonly applied to the skin in the belief that they cleansed the blood. The chemist would also make his own pills, sometimes having a simple pill machine, and powders would be measured out into individual doses and wrapped in small pre-cut sheets of paper. To a large extent the chemist was self-sufficient, although towards the latter end of the nineteenth century more proprietary brands of medicine became available, but it was not easy for the public to decide from advertisements which were genuine medicines and which were 'quack cures'.

It is interesting to note in newspaper advertisements that the chemist's shop often sold a wide range of goods that we would not today associate with such establishments. Taylors' Drug Co Ltd, a firm particularly strong in the area around Leeds, where towards the end of the century it had over a dozen shops, advertised themselves as 'The Great Cash Chemist, Patent Medicine Vendors, &c.' They supplied 'Pure drugs and chemicals, genuine patent medicines, proprietory articles, surgical appliances, perfumery and toilet requisites, homoeopathic medicines, soaps, brushes, combs, sponges, wash leathers, paints, oils

and varnishes.' This particular firm was keen to announce that prescriptions and family recipes are supplied at one-half the usual trade charges, and are dispensed with PURE DRUGS ONLY. Those sending for a price list were told that they 'would find a saving of $3\frac{1}{2}$d in the shilling can be effected'.

Not too far away, in James Street, Harrogate – 'The Bond Street of Harrogate' – visitors and residents would find Wilsons Ltd., The Modern Pharmacies (Atte ye signe of ye Hanging Syphon). In addition to high class dispensing they also offered a photographic dark-room, surgical appliances, and oxygen for lantern and inhalation.

As today, chemists towards the end of the period carried a wide range of proprietary medicine to meet individual needs. For rheumatism, lumbago and sprains, Elliman's Universal Embrocation was widely advertised – often next to an advertisement expounding its value as an essential item for the stable, and for the care of sheep, dogs and birds, whether they suffered from sprains, broken knees or sore throats! Many illnesses were regarded as being associated with impurities in the blood and Clarke's World-Famed Blood Mixture 'is warranted to cleanse the blood

"But be sure they are CARTER'S."

CARTER'S LITTLE LIVER PILLS are widely counterfeited. It is not enough to ask for "Little Liver Pills." CARTER is the important word, and should be observed on the outside wrapper; otherwise the Pills within cannot be genuine. Do not take any nameless "Little Liver Pills" that may be offered,

But be sure they are CARTER'S.

"RIDICULOUS!"

Ethel (who really thinks she must clean some of her old Gloves this Winter, times are so bad).
"DO YOU SELL KID-REVIVERS?"

Chemist. "YE—YES, M'M. I THINK YOU'LL FIND 'MRS. GUMMIDGE'S INFANT CORDIAL'
A MOST EXCEL——" [*Confusion.*

from all impurities from whatever cause arising'; a remedy for scurvy, eczema, bad legs, skin and blood diseases, pimples and sores of all kinds. It was advertised as 'the only real specific for gout and rheumatic pains, for it removes the cause from the blood and bones'.

Ensuring a good diet, particularly for children, in Victorian times cannot have been easy for those at the lower end of the social scale. We therefore find advertised a wide range of food products suitable to supplement normal meals for infants and invalids, among them Neave's Food, which the advertisement tells us is commended by Sir Charles A Cameron CB, MD, Ex-President of the Royal College of Surgeons, Ireland as being 'An Excellent Food admirably adapted to the Wants of Infants and Young Persons'. Another advertisement, for Frame Food, tell us that it is 'A Cooked Food rich in Albuminoids and Phosphates and therefore most nourishing for Infants, Invalids, and Everybody'. Benger's Food received a Gold

ABOVE: *The development of food supplements, especially for babies and children, could lead to confusion at the chemist's shop since he would also stock items like kid glove restorer!*
RIGHT: *Elliman's embrocation has been easing the aches of sportsmen for over a century!*

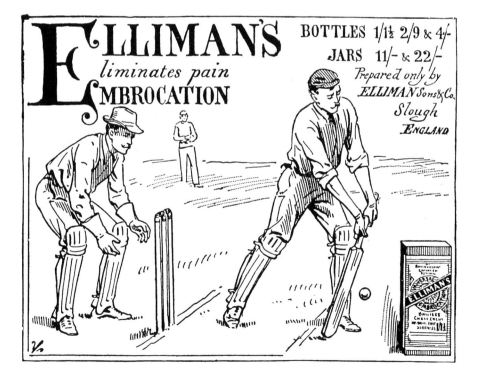

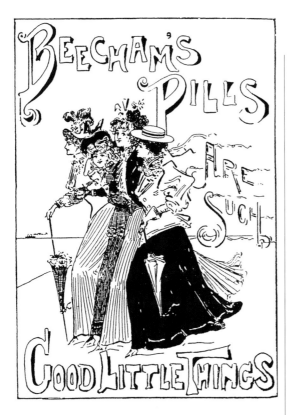

his goods, producing the *Beecham's Music Portfolio*, which he published for fifteen years; this was a booklet of popular songs for family entertainment, and sold seven million copies.

Jesse Boot was the son of an agricultural labourer who through ill health became a

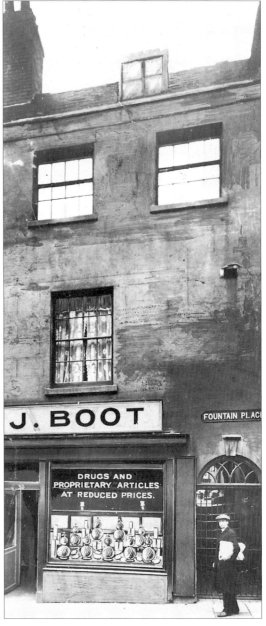

Medal at the Health Exhibition in London and the highest award at Adelaide in 1887.

Another well-known name to be found in the chemist's shop well over a hundred years ago was Beecham. Thomas Beecham had started to roll and powder pills in the 1840s at Kidlington, near Oxford. Here he learnt to mix the ingredients to form a stiff pliable mass which was then converted into pills by rolling on a marble slab and cutting the roll into strips. After final shaping, the pills were left to dry for several weeks before a coating was applied. After a short time he chose to become an itinerant pedlar selling such pills and this eventually led to him settling in Wigan where he spent one day a week manufacturing his remedies and the others selling them and keeping his books.

In 1858 he turned exclusively to manufacturing and selling, this gradually being to other chemists throughout the whole of the country. He used his love of music in the promotion of

FACING PAGE, LEFT: *An advertisement for Beecham's Pills directed at the fashionable female market.*
FACING PAGE, RIGHT: *Jesse Boot's famous claim to sell drugs and branded goods at prices people could afford.*
RIGHT: *The alternative to Boot's social conscience? Traditional druggists might prove too expensive for the Victorian underclass.*
BELOW: *Elliman's Embrocation was just as effective for veterinary aches and pains as those of humans.*

herbalist. After the death of Jesse Boot's father John, his widow, Mary, took over the little shop in Nottingham's Goose Gate where they sold soap, soda, camomile, senna, some household necessities and herbal remedies. When Jesse was thirteen he left school and went to help his mother, and in any spare moments he learned all he could about pharmacy.

In 1877, when Jesse was about twenty-seven, he took control of the shop. He was keen to sell drugs, proprietary items, and such necessities as candles at reduced prices, and he worked out how he could undercut the monopoly of the 'proper' chemists who had a

"AGAINST THE GRAIN."

Widow Woman (to Chemist, who was weighing a Grain of Calomel in dispensing a Prescription for her Sick Child). "MAN, YE NEEDNA' BE SAE SORIMPY WIT'—'TIS FOR A PUIR FATHERLESS BAIRN!"

price-fixing policy. Soon he was advertising in the *Nottingham Daily Express*, informing its readers of the 128 items he stocked – from Allen's Hair Restorer to Woodhouse's Rheumatic Elixir, and of course emphasizing the reduced prices. Other chemists were angered by his methods but within the first month his sales rose to £40 a week.

Jesse Boot sought to attract working-class people who could afford a few of the things he had on offer but he also had a real concern

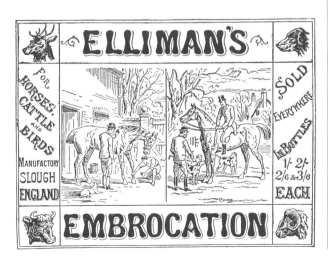

At that time, people could not take their prescriptions to the cut-price druggists, doctors had the monopoly on making up such medicines, but Jesse

for their well being, which originated from his Methodist upbringing and social conscience – later he renamed his shop 'The People's Store'.

As the business grew so he opened new premises, which he had designed himself. The frontage had plate-glass windows intersected by tastefully gilded spiralling columns. Inside the building there was a central office from which he could control the various departments and also a large workshop where Jesse's own proprietary items were made up – the forerunner of Boot's Own Brands.

employed a young qualified chemist and eventually he won the fight and reduced the charge for such medicines by half. His chain of ten shops now became 'Boots Cash Chemists' and J Boot & Co Ltd was formed.

The shop in Goose Gate was open until 9pm each evening, and until 11pm on Saturdays, and then there was the bookkeeping to do after that. At stocktaking time, when he had several branches, he would work right through every night for a fortnight – by the age of thirty-six Jesse Boot was worn out.

FACING PAGE, LEFT ABOVE & BELOW: *The poor diet of many Victorians made nutritional supplements, especially for babies and children, essential.*

FACING PAGE, BELOW RIGHT: *Elliman's truly was a 'universal embrocation', with advertising targeted at active women as well as men and animals!*

RIGHT: *Victorian parents were just as susceptible to advertising which engendered guilt for their lack of parental pride and concern as their twentieth-century counterparts.*

BELOW: *Advertisements in the new provincial towns were aimed at the fashionable clientele.*

BELOW RIGHT: *Another household name which has remained with us, Benger's Food was available at all chemists.*

While convalescing in Jersey he met Florence Rowe, the daughter of a local bookseller. They married and set up home in Nottingham and she started to play an increasingly important part in the business. It was Florence who encouraged him to devote a part of a few shops to stationery, artists' materials, other goods and also the circulating library. Boot's Book Lovers' Library charged borrowers 2d per book, and of course they had to pass the other counters to get to the library, no doubt remembering other needs as they passed the various displays!

By 1896 the company had sixty shops and a presence in twenty-eight towns. Thirty-five years later Florence Boot would open the 1000th Boots shop, but sadly Jesse Boot, Lord Trent of Nottingham, had died two years before.

The Cure-All
The Incredible Claims
of Victorian Advertisements

It is fascinating to sit down with a batch of Victorian magazines and just look at the classified and display advertisements. Not only did they claim remarkable properties for their goods, but the range of items on sale is almost unbelievable, especially considered in the light of today's health and safety concerns. How will people in a hundred years view our retailing, our goods?

Many are the pills and potions on offer – wonderful are the anticipated results! 'Parr's Life Pills – it is a fact beyond dispute that most

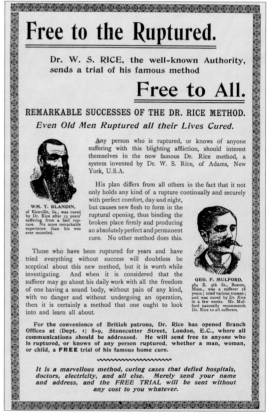

Free to the Ruptured.

Dr. W. S. RICE, the well-known Authority, sends a trial of his famous method

Free to All.

REMARKABLE SUCCESSES OF THE DR. RICE METHOD.
Even Old Men Ruptured all their Lives Cured.

Any person who is ruptured, or knows of anyone suffering with this blighting affliction, should interest themselves in the now famous Dr. Rice method, a system invented by Dr. W. S. Rice, of Adams, New York, U.S.A.

WM. T. BLANDIN, of Riceville, Ia., was cured by Dr. Rice after 33 years' suffering from a bad rupture. No more remarkable experience than his was ever recorded.

His plan differs from all others in the fact that it not only holds any kind of a rupture continually and securely with perfect comfort, day and night, but causes new flesh to form in the ruptural opening, thus binding the broken place firmly and producing an absolutely perfect and permanent cure. No other method does this.

Those who have been ruptured for years and have tried everything without success will doubtless be sceptical about this new method, but it is worth while investigating. And when it is considered that the sufferer may go about his daily work with all the freedom of one having a sound body, without pain of any kind, with no danger and without undergoing an operation, then it is certainly a method that one ought to look into and learn all about.

GEO. F. MULFORD, 484 E. 5th St., Boston, Mass., was a sufferer 18 years; tried various trusses; and was cured by Dr. Rice in a few weeks. Mr. Mulford naturally recommends Dr. Rice to all sufferers.

For the convenience of British patrons, Dr. Rice has opened Branch Offices at (Dept. 1) 8-9, Stonecutter Street, London, E.C., where all communications should be addressed. He will send free to anyone who is ruptured, or knows of any person ruptured, whether a man, woman, or child, a **FREE** trial of his famous home cure.

It is a marvellous method, curing cases that defied hospitals, doctors, electricity, and all else. Merely send your name and address, and the FREE TRIAL will be sent without any cost to you whatever.

AN ALARMING MESSAGE.
" IF YOU PLEASE, SIR, MOTHER'S TOOK THE LOTION, AND RUBBED
HER LEG WITH THE MIXTURE ! "

of the diseases with which the human race are afflicted are the result of a disordered state of the blood. To remedy this the occasional use of Parr's Life Pills should be had recourse to, and sickness prevented as well as cured, in their operation they go straight to the disease . . . Sold in boxes at 1s 1½d, 2s 9d, and family packets at 11s each, by all respectable medicine vendors throughout the world. Full directions are given with each box.' This is a classified advertisement in *The Illustrated*

Mrs S.A.ALLEN'S
World's

Hair Restorer.

IS PERFECTION!
For restoring Grey, White, or Faded
Hair to its youthful Colour, Gloss, and
Beauty. It renews its life, strength,
and growth. Dandruff quickly re-
moved. A matchless Hair Dressing
Its perfume rich and rare.

London News in 1850 – obviously good health does not come cheap, bearing in mind the low wages of the day.

Or Du Barry's Revalenta Arabica Food may answer your need – for it claims that it is: 'A nice, safe, and effectual remedy for Indigestion, Constipation, Acidity, Heartburn, Flatulency, Distension, Palpitation, Debility, Nervous, Bilious, and Liver Complaints, Nausea and Sickness during Pregnancy, &c. Copies of testimonials of 50,000 cures gratis. In canisters, with instructions, 1lb., 2s 9d, . . . 12lb., 22s.' This marvellous food was available from the manufacturer or from all grocers and chemists.

Alternatively, in the same issue, if you have problems with your teeth then here is your remedy: 'The Teeth – A very curious new invention connected with Dental Surgery has been introduced by Mr. Howard of 17, George Street, Hanover Square; it is the introduction of an entirely new description of Artificial Teeth, fixed without springs, wires or ligatures. They so perfectly resemble natural teeth, as not to be distinguished from the originals by the closest observer. They will never change colour or decay, and will be found very superior to any teeth ever before used. This method does not require the extraction of

roots, or any painful operation, and will support and preserve the teeth that are loose, and is guaranteed to restore articulation and mastication . . .' Another company interested in the care of teeth advertises 'Metcalfe and Co.'s New Pattern Tooth-Brush – The Tooth-Brush searches thoroughly into the divisions, and cleanses them in the most extraordinary manner, hairs never come loose: 1s.'

Earlier, in 1844, if 'Stooping of the Shoulders' be your problem then the 'Patent St. James's Chest Expander' may be for you – the advertisement claims that 'This invisible, comfortable and most successful means of imparting a healthful and graceful expansion of the figure, which is used in the families of eminent medical gentlemen, and by persons of all ages, is sent per post . . .' For ladies with 'Pimples, Spots, Blotches, Redness, Tan, Freckles, and other defects of the Skin' then Rowland's Kalydor is for them because 'The

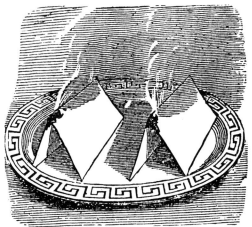

CIGARS DE JOY
ASTHMA
COUGH · BRONCHITIS

These **CIGARETTES** give immediate relief in the worst attack of ASTHMA, COUGH, CHRONIC BRONCHITIS, INFLUENZA, and SHORTNESS of BREATH. Persons who suffer at night with coughing, phlegm, and short breath, find them invaluable, as they instantly check the spasm, promote sleep, and allow the patient to pass a good night. They are perfectly harmless, and may be smoked by ladies, children, and most delicate patients.

In Boxes of 35 Cigarettes, 2/6, from all Chemists and Stores. Each genuine box bears the name WILCOX & CO., 239, Oxford Street, London. Post-free.

OZONE PAPER
For the Relief and Cure of
ASTHMA,
CHRONIC BRONCHITIS, and
BRONCHITIC ASTHMA.

HARRISON WEIR, Esq., writes:—" I not only use the Ozone Paper myself, but I recommend it to all Asthmatics I meet with as the best remedy for their complaint."

Mr. WOODWARD, Worcester, writes:—" I have derived more permanent benefit from using your Ozone Paper than anything I have tried, and found the same with regard to my asthmatic patients."

2s. 9d. and 4s. 6d. per box, of all Chemists ; or from the Proprietor for the amount in stamps or P.O O. to any country within the Postal Union.
R. HUGGINS, Chemist, 199, Strand, LONDON.

radiant bloom it imparts to the Cheek, and the softness and delicacy it induces on the hands, arms, and neck render it indispensable to every toilet' and 'As a safeguard against Chilblains and Chapped Skin its virtues are universally acknowledged.' What more could you want? – and it was patronised and sanctioned by Her Majesty the Queen, the Royal Family, and several courts of Europe!

Moving to 1888 we find, in *The Graphic*, the Medico-Electric Belt, Truss and Battery Co, Limited of New Bond Street in London

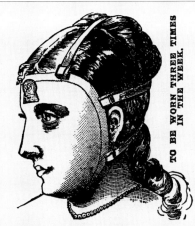

Madame H. M. ROWLEY'S
TOILET MASK
(Or Face Glove)

TO BE WORN THREE TIMES IN THE WEEK.

Is a **natural beautifier** for **bleaching** and **preserving** the **skin** and **removing complexional imperfections.**

It is **soft** and **flexible** in form, and can be **worn** without **discomfort** or **inconvenience.**

It is recommended by eminent physicians and scientists as a substitute for injurious cosmetics.

COMPLEXION BLEMISHES may be hidden imperfectly by cosmetics and powders, but can only be removed permanently by the Toilet Mask. By its use every kind of spots, impurities, roughness, etc., vanish from the skin, leaving it soft, clear, brilliant, and beautiful. It is harmless, costs little, and saves pounds uselessly expended, for cosmetics, powders, lotions, etc. It prevents and removes wrinkles, and is both a complexion preserver and beautifier. Illustrated Treatise post free two stamps. Address, and kindly mention this Magazine—

Mrs. H. M. ROWLEY,
THE TOILET MASK CO., 139, OXFORD STREET, LONDON, W.

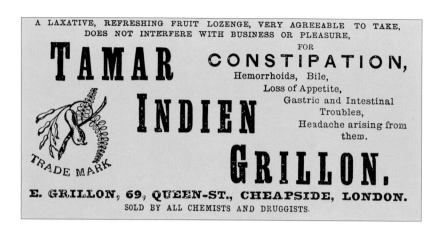

offering Johnson's Hygio-Electric Belt which combines 'the well-known efficacy of a portable Voltaic Battery of unique construction, with the hygienic properties of Dr Daubigne's Medicated Pumilio Pinol Felt.' It is 'A boon to the afflicted, a speedy and reliable cure for Rheumatism, Sciatica, Lumbago, Gout, Indigestion, Paralysis, Epilepsy, Liver Complaints, Nervous Debility and every form of Nervous or Organic Derangement.' Amazing! Further

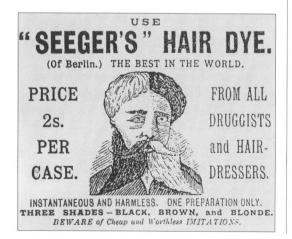

on we find that 'Cigars de Joy' are cigarettes which 'give immediate relief in the worst attack of Asthma, Cough, Chronic Bronchitis, Influenza, and Shortness of Breath . . . They are perfectly harmless, and may be smoked by ladies, children, and most delicate patients.' They were available in boxes of 35 cigarettes for 2s 6d.

For those suffering from toothache 'Tikheel' would seem to be the cure. An advertisement tells us that this remedy, available from chemists, 'is a new discovery, quite harmless when taken as directed, absolutely free from Morphia, Opium, or any preparation of the kind . . . the proprietors have every confidence in recommending it . . . as a most valuable medicine for safely, speedily, and certainly curing one of the most common but painful classes of disease. Tikheel at once removes the Tooth-ache to which Females are at times so peculiarly subject. One Dose rapidly removes the terrible pains arising from Neuralgia in the head, Face-Ache and Tooth-Ache, even when proceeding from a decayed tooth, rendering extraction unnecessary'!

Each week, each year, each magazine seems to have something different on offer. 'The Tafilalt Elixir, or Doctor Assoulin's Hooping [sic] Cough Mixture' claims to cure asthma, influenza, shortness of breath, and all diseases of the lungs. However if you are suffering from Indigestion, Lassitude (Weariness), Heartburn or Feverish Colds, then take Lamplugh's Pyretic Saline – which also prevents and quickly relieves or cures the worst form of Typhus, Scarlet, Jungle, and other Fevers, Prickly Heat, Small-pox, Measles, Eruptive or Skin Complaints, and various other altered conditions of the Blood!

In *The Illustrated London News* of 1844 is a hair treatment recommended by a chemist in Whitby, Yorkshire who had written to the manufacturers in 1841: 'Gentlemen, Of the last supply of Oldridge's Balm of Columbia, every bottle was sold on receipt, and I have many more bespoke, only waiting for a further supply, which I hope you will send without the least delay. Orders have poured in . . . since the powerful effects of the balm have been so decisively demonstrated . . . A gentleman who had had little or no hair for twenty years, who had had his head shaved and wore a wig . . . tried the balm and after using it according to the directions for a short time, the young hair appeared

and he has now as fine a head of hair as any person in Whitby. Yours, &c, John Kilvington.' The manufacturers went on to claim that Oldridge's Balm prevents the hair turning grey, and the first application causes it to curl beautifully, frees it from scurf, and stops it falling off.

Life must have been good for, seemingly, every ill could cured by taking a pill, wearing an electric belt or smoking a Cigar de Joy!

Boots, Shoes and Clogs

Throughout most of the years of Queen Victoria's reign many people had their shoes made by a bespoke shoemaker, it was only the working class who bought ready-made shoes from a multiple shop. Clogs were commonly worn by working-class folk, particularly those of the northern mill towns, and such people would only buy new footwear once a year, in time for the Sunday School processions or the annual seaside holiday. Most villages had a shoemaker and cobbler who met the needs

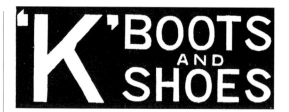

of the local population. Some of the unfortunate 'street-urchins' often went bare-footed and many poor people wore the cast offs of the 'better offs'.

The bespoke shoemaker used individual lasts, fashioned to the size and shape of the feet of each particular customer; the boots and shoes of the multiple shop, in those early days, did not give such detail as we expect today. The shop window would be filled with every available style of boot and shoe, with no eye for layout or interest. Cheaper, unboxed boots and shoes were generally held together with string threaded through a stiffener, and these were displayed on rods or rails in the shop doorways.

Already some footwear was made using a combination of factory processes and out-workers. In other instances, 'cottage industry' shoemakers bought leather from merchants

FACING PAGE: *William Timpson progressed from bootlace-maker at eight years old to proprietor of 26 shops and a factory by 1896.*
RIGHT: *An eye-catching window display of ladies' and gentlemens' boots and shoes.*
BELOW: *Young's shoe polish promises 'Perfection'!*

and then sold back the finished shoes which were sold on to shoe shops. The Somervell brothers operated in both these ways in Kendal, on the edge of the Lake District. However, they found that some of those who bought leather from them were selling back shoes made of inferior leather, and that the higher quality leather was being sold elsewhere. To prevent this they started to stamp their leather with the letter 'K', the initial letter of the town of Kendal, and so the famous trademark was created. It wasn't until the 1930s that they became involved in shoe retailing.

Henry Quant opened his shoe shop at 29 Abbeygate Street, Bury St Edmunds in 1798 and, following his death, the shop was run by his widow and son William. Unfortunately they had a severe disagreement and William opened up next door in opposition to his

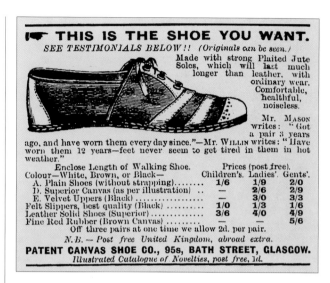

mother. He was very successful and eventually bought her shop. In 1850 he opened a branch in Newmarket, and about 1858 moved

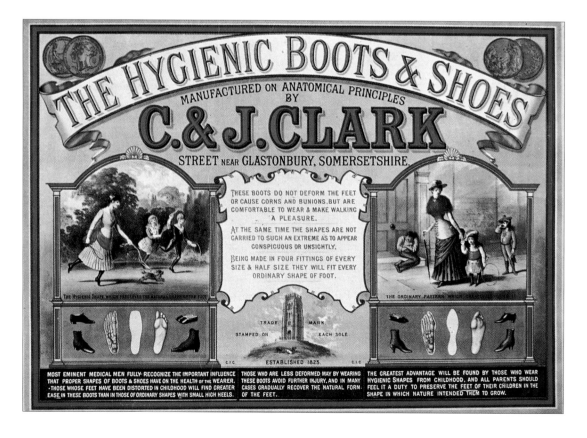

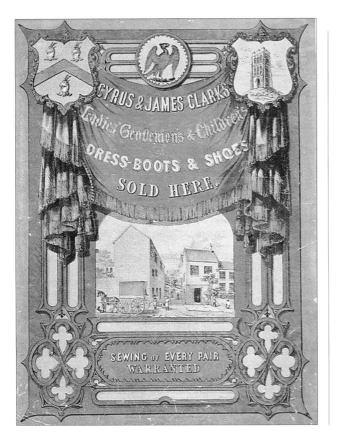

premises in Bury St Edmunds to 49 Abbeygate Street.

He was one of the first in the town to supply ready-made boots, although he did also sell bespoke boots. Meanwhile in Norwich, a town renowned for its involvement in the shoe trade, James Smith had started making ladies' shoes, in the Upper Market, somewhere near the Guildhall. The firm was later taken over by

FACING PAGE, ABOVE: *Buying shoes by mail order was possible, as this advertisement shows.*

BELOW: *Clark's shoes promised footcare with every size and half-size of boot and shoe made in four fittings, bringing the principles of hand-made bootmaking to the ready-made shoe trade.*

ABOVE LEFT: *Clark's shoes and boots always offered superior quality with sewing of every pair 'warranted'.*

ABOVE RIGHT: *The London Shoe Company offered boots on approbation.*

RIGHT: *The satirists noted that ladies were keen on fashion before comfort and durability.*

A POSER.

"IT'S NOT SO MUCH A *DURABLE* ARTICLE THAT I REQUIRE, MR. CRISPIN. I WANT SOMETHING *DAINTY*, YOU KNOW—SOMETHING *COY*, AND AT THE SAME TIME JUST A WEE BIT *SAUCY!*"

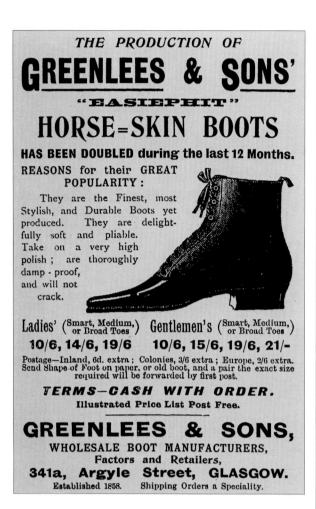
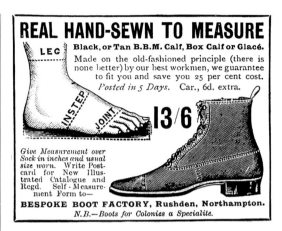
would in later days have over 200 shops, a shoe factory, 30 shoe repair factories, and employ 3,500 people.

William Timpson was not a man of robust health, and from an early age became increasingly deaf, but he worked very hard, and virtually had to retire when he was only thirty-one. He was the youngest of six children of a silkweaver and was born in 1849 in Rothwell, Northamptonshire. William had little formal education and by the age of eight was making leather bootlaces. He also carried boots for outworkers to Mr Gotch's factory in Kettering, where army boots were manufactured. Whilst still a youngster, perhaps only aged ten or eleven, he went by train to Manchester where his eldest brother Charles lived, and for whom he delivered boots. However, he later returned to Rothwell to learn the art of shoe making before once again going back to Manchester to form the partnership with Walter Joyce. William Timpson was then only sixteen years old.

Four years later when William opened his own shop at 97 Oldham Street he paid £200 a year rental, a lot of money at that time,

Charles Winter, before passing into the hands of Willis and Southall in 1865. Today's generation of shoppers would recognize their brand name 'Start-rite', but it was a name created by Quant & Son for a patent design of children's shoes in 1921 and later sold to Willis and Southall.

William Timpson and his brother-in-law Walter Joyce traded at 298 Oldham Road, Manchester, from 1865. However the real foundation of Timpsons, as we know it today, dates from April 1869 when William Timpson opened a shop at 97 Oldham Street, in the centre of Manchester, under his own name; it was the first shop of a business which

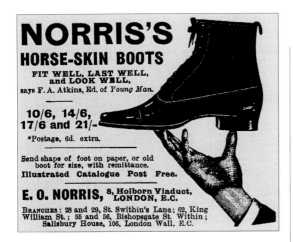
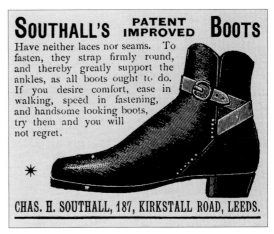
indeed some thought it would prove ruinous to his business. The building was probably about a hundred years old and in a very poor state. He spent all his savings on shopfittings and obtained his initial stock footwear from William Shaw of Dantzic Street, Manchester, who had known him as a Sunday School worker at Ashley Lane church, and trusted him implicitly.

Boots in those days were made of French Calf, Kips or Splits and were very difficult to polish for display – many hours were spent doing this task. To ensure shoes kept their shape in the window they were filled with crinkled paper – fancy coloured paper or old gold silk was used in the top of ladies' shoes. Each pair had a price ticket, which often obscured the potential customer's view of the shoes. Soon people were coming from miles around to visit Number 97, and William claimed that on many Saturdays not only had he sold over 100 pairs of men's boots, but he had personally served each customer! The hours were long and it was not uncommon for shops such as his to open on a Sunday morning for customers to exchange the boots they had bought the previous day.

Inside shops like William's were long rows of gas pipes, fitted with jets, which ran the length of the building, and from these pipes hung hundreds of pairs of children's shoes. The shops were often dingy and gloomy for the lighting was poor, and they also smelt of leather and a kind of size, which was made

of gum dragon, kid reviver and ink, and which was used on the pairs placed in the shop window – it caused a permanent stain on the staff's hands. The staff usually consisted of a manager, a young lady and also a junior girl, plus the errand boy; larger shops might have two or three sales ladies and even other men on the staff. The manager wore the traditional shoemaker's apron, whilst women assistants wore tight fitting black dresses which were shiny and decorated with satin; in Manchester their hair was usually full of curling pins, which were hidden under their hats!

LEFT: *Moscovite Lustre shoe polish must have been a welcome addition to the range available with its claim to be self-polishing.* ABOVE: *Comfort or fashion? Walking shoes or high-fashion boots, the same dilemma faces ladies and gentlemen choosing footwear today!* FACING PAGE: *The interior of a Victorian shoe shop stacked high from floor to ceiling with boots and shoes.*

Most of the shops were single premises with one large window and a door to the side of it. The window display was divided down the centre with men's goods on one side and ladies' on the other. The shopfront was generally of polished mahogany in better branches, and painted wood in poorer shops. Each shop had a glazed sign or name plate with the lettering engraved on the wooden framework or painted on the glass. Window backs often consisted of silvered mirrors to reflect the window display.

When William Timpson was twenty-three he married Elizabeth Farey, started to live over the shop, and it was here that his daughter was born. His father-in-law was Kettering's first photographer, in 1860.

By 1896 Timpsons had twenty-six shops and a factory which produced 750 pairs of men's boots a week. It was however still a private business and William Timpson was the sole owner. Timpsons in Oldham Street was still the principal shop and the distribution warehouse adjoined it. Other better-class shops were towards the south of Manchester, and those supplying working-class customers were on the main routes leading out towards Salford and surrounding districts.

Initially, boots and shoes were distributed to shops which were within a two-mile radius of Oldham Street by the errand lad, who used a sack-barrow as his means of transport; to take goods further afield Timpsons employed a local green-grocer. In 1898 they acquired their own horse and wagon.

Down in the West Country, Quaker brothers Cyrus and James Clark had started to make shoes and socks. They travelled far and wide across the country selling their goods, and as early as 1836 one-third of their footwear was exported to Ireland; they did not employ a salesman until 1849. In 1842 they produced 12,000 pairs of footwear, each one given a maker's number as part of their system of checking quality. It was not until 1856 that sewing machines were introduced into their factory – three treadle machines supplied by Isaac Singer. By the 1860s other machines had been bought and adapted to allow the use of waxed threads, so essential to ensure that

heavy waterproof boots 'keep the feet dry and warm, in spite of dews and wet grass'. By 1880 ready-made shoes had come to stay, not least due to trade received from the women and children of the greatly enlarged middle class. In 1883 Clarks advertised on posters 'The Hygienic Boots & Shoes', claiming 'These boots do not deform the feet or cause corns and bunions, but are comfortable to wear and make walking a pleasure.' Every size and half size was made in four fittings to ensure they would 'fit every ordinary shape of foot'.

Other shoe shops familiar with twentieth century shoppers, which were also well-known names in the second half of Queen Victoria's reign, include Lilley & Skinner which was founded in 1842, and Freeman Hardy & Willis which was started by Edward Wood in Leicester in 1870.

In 1825 Thomas Lilley had started to make shoes in King Street, Borough, London, and was one of the first shoemakers to combine wholesale and retail trade; above the shops he put up the board 'Thos Lilley'. Over the next thirty years other factories were opened; the firm were pioneers in the machine production of shoes. It wasn't until 1870 that Thomas Lilley jnr. entered the business, but shortly afterwards he left with one of the sales representatives, W Banks Skinner, who was also his brother-in-law. In 1881 the pair formed a partnership and the name 'Lilley & Skinner' appeared over the shops. Later father and son were reconciled and the companies amalgamated, becoming a private company in 1894. Two of the company's early brands were 'Sensible' and 'Perfect' shoes.

When Edward Wood decided to turn his business into a limited company he became its chairman and appointed as directors William Freeman who was his factory manager, Arthur Hardy who was an architect, and Frederick Willis who was his traveller – Freeman, Hardy & Willis Ltd! While Freeman and Willis did not remain directors for very long the Hardy family connection lasted until 1953. By 1877 the company had decided to concentrate on the retail aspect of the business and closed down its factory; by 1900 Freeman Hardy & Willis had 300 branches.

LEFT: A Punch cartoon capturing the indecisiveness that increased choice engendered.

Fireside Shopping

The term 'Fireside Shopping' was created and registered by Ellwood Brockbank who had 'The Warehouse' in Settle, a Yorkshire Dales market town. We tend to think that mail order shopping is an invention of the twentieth century, but it was clearly a major way in which goods were purchased throughout the whole of the Victorian era. Many of the national and regional weekly and monthly magazines of the period carried very extensive display and small advertisements for an unbelievably wide range of goods and services, many of which were available direct from the manufacturers or through their appointed agents.

Ellwood Brockbank, who was born in 1841, came from a Salford Quaker family. When his father died in 1854 he had to leave Ackworth School, near Wakefield, and in 1855,

he obtained a job with the Quaker firm of John Tatham & Son in Settle. Tatham's was something like a department store, for in addition to selling groceries it also sold a range of druggists' products, as well as hosiery and drapery. It sold bibles, as well, for it was a depot of the British & Foreign Bible Society. The family business specialised in Yorkshire hams and bacon, produced from locally raised and cured pigs, and Wensleydale cheeses, some weighing as much as 15lbs.

Eventually, while still working for Tatham's, Ellwood Brockbank opened separate premises behind the shops, and here he pioneered his shopping by post. His system was heartily recommended by a trade paper of the 1880s. He was said to be 'the inaugurator of a useful system for the distribution of goods at wholesale prices to retail customers throughout the country'; the Brockbank system was also a way of shopping without leaving home, and in 1897, *The Lady* magazine also applauded the advantages 'of being enabled to have goods straight from the manufactory – no Middleman's prices intervening, the goods too, being of the latest style and value'.

He concentrated on just three textile firms to supply all his needs – dress fabrics from William Ecroyd & Sons near Burnley in Lancashire, serges from Fox Brothers & Co. at Wellington in Somerset and for linens, J. N. Richardsons & Owden Ltd. in Belfast. Ellwood produced boxes of patterns which he sent free to enquirers, but when goods were ordered it was strictly on a cash only basis, with no discount! Goods were sent by

carriage, by return, or were sent postage paid to all parts of Britain. Ellwood Brockbank was never tempted to open a shop and only ever had the one address, 'The Warehouse, Settle'.

A very different form of home shopping had arrived in 1868, when a new weekly newspaper specializing in this area was published. *The Bazaar, Exchange and Mart, and Journal of the Household* was later to be published every Monday, Wednesday and Friday, price 2d. The publishers claimed that its success was due to a 'hitherto almost unknown, or at any rate unrecognised, trait in the human race – its ineradicable love of bargains and trafficking.' Until then, it had been assumed, they continued, that if people traded at all, they did it from necessity as a pure matter of business, and not merely for the fun of the thing. The *Pall Mall Gazette*, commented on the large number of transactions which took place through the paper: 'More than 10,000 announcements appear weekly in its columns.' In addition to the advertisements, the paper by

1890, also contained 'high-class literary matter', articles on art topics, which included notices of exhibitions and artists and their works, music and drama, and 'such subjects as are discussed in the Drawing Room'; sport, travel, cage birds and photography, outdoor and men's subjects, ones discussed in the Hall; fashions and etiquette, and generally topics that only concern ladies, ones that are discussed in the Boudoir; cookery and confectionery and the

management of children – items for the House-keeper's Room, along with items to do with the garden, dogs, horses, etc.

It seems little was too big to be bought by mail order, for in the *Fortnightly Review* in 1883, Oetzmann & Co. of Hampstead Road in London offer Club Divan easy chairs, double sprung, stuffed with best hair and finished very soft for £5 5s, 'orders per post receive prompt and faithful attention.' Heal's of Tottenham Court Road also carried out an extensive delivery service, to service their mail order catalogue. As the railways developed, so Heal's used them to transport their goods and also advertised in the stations. They encouraged potential customers to visit their premises and announced their catalogue – the 1852 one offered 67 patterns of iron and brass bedsteads and cribs as well as a wide range of furniture, not only for the important rooms of the house, but also for those of the servants.

John Noble Ltd. of Brook Street Mills, Manchester, who advertised itself as the largest firm of costumiers in the world, offered to send patterns post free 'to all who name *The Strand Magazine*'. Readers were offered 'A box of 1000 patterns of winter dress goods . . . LENT to select from, and sent carriage paid.' Other companies generally made similar offers.

Shopping in Rural Areas

I t is very easy to dwell on what was happening in our cities and towns during the nineteenth century and forget that some people never ventured further than their own village or the nearest market town; this perhaps being especially so for those living in areas like the Lake District, the remoter parts of the Yorkshire Dales or Cornwall.

In *The Sandboys*, the adventures of a family who went to the Great Exhibition from their home in Buttermere in the Lake District, we see several examples of what rural life was like in what at that time must have been a very isolated part of the country, some 300 miles from the capital.

Today, Buttermere is still a tranquil and beautiful place, only a matter of minutes away from bustling Keswick in a car; back then, it was the peripatetic grocer who travelled the ten miles and came to the cottagers with his pony and cart. There was no grocer between Buttermere and Keswick and people relied on Matthew Harker 'for t' tea, and sugar, and soft bread'. The villagers had subscribed with others of the gentry to enable Matthew to start his little travelling business, after he had lost a hand when blasting cobbles.

It was just the same if you were ill, it was ten miles to the nearest doctor or chemist, and Buttermere also had no baker, no butcher, no

bookseller, confectioner nor pawnbroker –
it was even six miles to post a letter! Impro-
visation had often to be the order of the day;
a bedside lamp could be made from bacon
fat, using a length of darning cotton as a wick.

It was, however, to Keswick that the villagers
would go when it was the Keswick Cheese
Fair at Martinmas time; throughout the rest of
the year, it was the weekly Monday market at
Cockermouth that took Christopher (or, after
the Cumberland fashion, 'Cursty') Sandboys
and his wife away from their solitary life.

Some villages were lucky enough to have
a village shop. In it would be found bread,
cheese, bacon, tea, ribbons, tape, shoes and a
hundred and one other things – as multifarious
as a bazaar. Behind and above the shop, the
storekeeper and his family would live and
perhaps make things like 'pricked' rugs that
they could sell, although many villagers would
make such things themselves on dark winter
evenings. In larger villages there would be the
butcher's shop and the bakery, the draper and
the hardware store – all serving the needs of
not only the local community, but the far flung
neighbours living on isolated farms, the railway
workers or the men building the reservoir.

PREVIOUS PAGE: *Prittlewell village shop in 1891, a mecca for
children with its tins of biscuits and jars of sticky sweets.*
BELOW: The Farm Market *by Francis Donkin Bedford,
from 'The Book of Shops', 1899.*
FACING PAGE: The Village Shop, *1887, by James Charles.*

In many aspects of life, village people were self-sufficient, growing their own vegetables on small strips of land, perhaps even having the odd pig, or two or three sheep, and bartering the results of their labour. Village women would bake and knit and sew, they were multi-talented. Life was not easy, but it was often richer than that of the town-dweller.

The Departmental Store

The development of transport within towns and cities, and the growth of the railway system between them, were perhaps the chief factors which led to the founding of department stores. 'Omnibuses' allowed people to go from shop to shop in various parts of the town, or in central London, to find the goods they wanted and to compare prices. The Great Exhibition of 1851 led to a great increase in omnibuses and by 1853 there were 3,000 horse omnibuses in London; three years later the small omnibus companies were absorbed by the French General Omnibus Company of London and regular services were now assured. However, at the time, fares were too expensive for the working class, and therefore the gentle-folk need not fear being contaminated by such people on this new mode of transport!

In 1863 the first underground station was opened, the Metropolitan Railway, which linked the City to the West End, and also to Paddington Railway Station.

In many parts of the country the population of towns and cities, particularly industrial ones in the Midlands and the north of England, were increasing at a fast rate. (Although in the City of London, the residential population fell from 128,000 in 1851 to 75,000 in 1871.) As such changes occurred, the value of land and property in city centres grew, and rents and rates soared. Shop-keepers realized that instead of acquiring adjacent properties when wishing to expand, now they must use the upper floors of premises as selling space. This gave the opportunity for the creation of individual departments, and in 1870 Debenham & Freebody had twenty-seven which included coloured silks, black silks, furs, costumes, dresses, parasols, household drapery, and embroidered muslins. In earlier times these rooms had been used as hostels for staff who lived on the premises, and for work rooms and offices; such functions were now accommodated in premises in less expensive properties in nearby side-streets.

LEFT: *Ladies and gentlemen could expect goods to be brought out to their carriages so they could choose in comfort and not have to carry their purchases.*
FACING PAGE, ABOVE: *An advertisement for Brixton's Bon Marché, the first purpose-built department store in England.*
BELOW: *Bon Marché's window display packed with an assortment of goods.*

'Window-shopping', and the idea of having a day's shopping in town had begun, although early window displays were certainly not artistic, for they were filled with as much merchandise as possible, from back to front and from floor to ceiling.

Brixton's Bon Marché was the first store in England to be purpose built as a department store, rather than growing from a small draper's, silk mercer's or haberdasher's; a few others, such as Harrods and Fortnum & Mason, grew from grocery shops. It is now difficult to imagine such stores without electric light, lifts and escalators, electronic tills and all the developments of the twentieth century, but let us look at life as it was.

Arnold Bennett's *The Old Wives' Tale*, set in the early 1860s, tells of Mrs Baines's shop where three dwelling houses had been converted into one to make Baines's drapery shop: 'The showroom was over the millinery and silken half of the shop. Over the woollen and shirting half were the drawing-room and the chief bedroom. When in quest of articles of coquetry, you mounted from the shop by a curving stair, and your head gradually rose level with a large apartment having a mahogany counter in front of the window and along one side, yellow linoleum on the floor, many cardboard boxes, a magnificent hinged cheval glass, and two chairs.' Downstairs there was a central cash

desk from which Mrs Baines could survey the whole shop.

A man with ambition was Frank Bentall who left his native Essex, gained experience in Southampton and then, in 1867, took over Mr Hatt's drapery shop at 31 Clarence Street, Kingston upon Thames. Mr Hatt, his family, three men assistants and a servant had all lived in the small rooms over the shop and Frank Bentall knew what to expect, for his father was a draper in Maldon where his family and shop assistants had also lived above the shop.

The centre of trade in the town was the market place, but Clarence Street, a mix of cottages, inns and a few small shops, was on the fringe. It was extremely narrow, barely wide enough for two stage coaches to pass one another, and visited only by Hansom cabs and similar vehicles because in the 1860s there was no public transport – the horse-drawn tram did not appear until 1870 and the bicycle was still unknown. The footpaths of the town were poor or non-existent, and the cobbled streets were frequently covered in mud. However, Clarence Street had one major advantage – it was on the direct approach to the bridge over the Thames, and therefore attracted much trade.

In the middle of the nineteenth century there were twenty-five drapers' shops in Kingston, then only a small country town, but for those who could afford fine dresses, the crinoline fashions of the day required many yards of fabric and ribbons, which meant good business for the drapers.

In those days it was common practice for the proprietor of the shop to greet his customers as they entered his premises. He would know most of them by name as they

were loyal, often over several generations. Similarly such family businesses received many years of service from employees, it being not uncommon for someone to give over fifty years continuous service to one employer – Bentalls' chief cashier gave fifty-two years, and the boot and shoe buyer forty-nine years.

Shop hours in the 1860s at Bentalls were from 8am to 9pm, or even 10pm but added to these hours would be the preparatory time when brasses must be cleaned and displays checked, and after closing there was tidying up to be done. At Christmas 1868, when Christmas Day was on a Friday, the staff also received Boxing Day and the Sunday as holiday – three consecutive days, a real breakthrough. In 1890, however, Frank Bentall started to close the shop at 5pm on Wednesdays, the forerunner of the modern early-closing day, and by now closing time on other days had moved to 8pm, apart from Saturdays.

Over the years, little by little, Bentalls acquired adjoining properties and extended its range of departments to include millinery, hosiery, costumes and jackets, ladies' and children's underwear, and fabrics. It had a busy

FACING PAGE: *Oxford Circus, 1842, by Thomas Shotter Boys.*
ABOVE: *The latest fashion showing 'gunmetal' embroidery.*
BELOW: *This poster advertising Spencer, Turner & Boldero is a lithoprint, dating from 1865.*

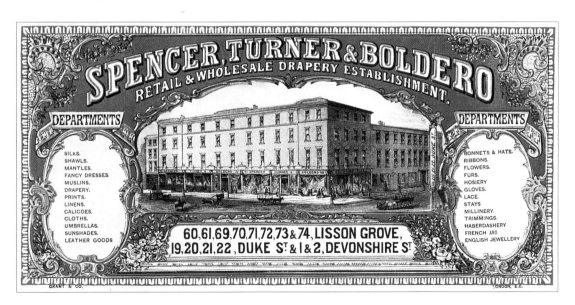

dressmaking department as at that time very few clothes were ready-to-wear, and other additions were departments for carpets and matting, and one for mourning – a must in the days of formal mourning and high death rates. Indeed if the draper called round to measure up the family for mourning clothes it was not unusual for him to be asked if he would like to 'pay his own last respects to the deceased'.

By the turn of the century Bentalls had taken over four adjacent properties and was on its way to becoming one of the region's best-known department stores.

James Jolly was over fifty when he came to Bath, and had already traded in Margate and London's New Bond Street. 'Economy, Fashion and Variety' were the distinguishing features of Jolly and Son's Emporium at 11 and 12 Milsom Street in 1831, or so claimed the advertisements. However, the shop also had an 'exclusive Ready Money System, no Article being delivered unless upon prompt payment', and the advertisement also warned customers that 'There will be no abatement made from the price asked, the profit on each article being too small to admit of any reduction.'

Wealthy people from all over the country came to the Spa to take their cures at the baths and Pump Room, and were also attracted by the town's quality shops. Milsom Street was Bath's most fashionable residential street, so Jolly's partners and buyers went direct to the weavers in France, Italy and Switzerland for their silks. From those early days of the 1830s onward the store boasted linen drapery, silk mercery, hosiery, haberdashery, shawls, merinos, lace nets etc. The Bazaar department also offered foreign china and bijouterie, alabaster clocks, Italian alabaster urns, vases, and figures, British and foreign cabinet goods, jewellery, perfumery, stationery, combs, brushes, cutlery, toys, and almost all the multifarious articles usually kept in bazaars. Samples and catalogues would be sent to the homes of visitors and orders could be placed by post – at that time a 14-yard dress length of heavy black corded silk would be used to make an ordinary afternoon dress, the work being done by

FACING PAGE: *The exterior of Harrod's department store, 1892.*
RIGHT & BELOW: *The provisions department and Food Hall at Harrods.*

the lady's own dressmaker. However, towards the end of the century ladies were offered ready-made 'Irish hand-embroidered' white linen nightdresses for 2s 11½d.

Although today we think of Harrods as perhaps the masterpiece of British retailing, back in the 1850s it was only a small grocery business run by its founder, Charles Henry Harrod, then in his fifties, who lived over the shop in Brompton Road.

In 1861 Charles Digby Harrod, C H Harrod's son, took over the business, having had to buy it from his father. He appreciated the way in which the area was developing, partly

stimulated by the Great Exhibition of 1851, but also by the building of houses in Knightsbridge, mansions in Cromwell Road, and the promise of permanent museums in South Kensington. By 1867 he had increased his assistants to five and had also installed a new shopfront, complete with a plate-glass window, and his name in gold letters on elaborate wire-blinds. By the end of 1868 his turnover had grown to £1,000 a week.

Now the store started to expand as he moved his family to live in Esher, using the previous living accommodation to provide extra salesrooms and storerooms. With his cousin, William Kibble, helping him, he started to stock extra lines such as perfumes, stationery and patent medicines, all at low prices, following the example of the Co-operative movement. By 1870 he was employing sixteen staff and that year issued a 65-page catalogue. Further expansion of the premises was achieved when he built a two-storey extension over the back garden and gradually he acquired the leases of 101 and 103 Brompton Road. Now he started selling cooked meat and game, fruit, flowers, vegetables, confectionery and china – and of course a delivery van had become essential.

Harrod was a hard taskmaster, but a just one. By 1880 he was employing almost a hundred people, all of whom lived out; however for every quarter-of-an-hour they were late they were fined 1½d! On 6 December 1883 the business could have been doomed to disaster for a terrible fire destroyed the whole premises. However, Charles Harrod masterminded the operation from the back room of a nearby public house, sent orders to his suppliers for new supplies, and also wrote to his customers that: 'your order will be delayed in the execution of a day or two'. Harrod's Christmas trade for 1883 beat all previous records.

His new store was opened in September 1884 with several new innovations, among them the 'Pay Desk'. Several cash desks were put in and customers were directed to pay at them after they had chosen their goods.

FACING PAGE & THIS PAGE
RIGHT: *Bainbridge &
Co Ltd, Newcastle on
Tyne; the grand
showrooms opened
in July 1898.*
BELOW: *Francis Donkin
Bedford*, The Haber-
dasher *from 'The
Book of Shops', 1899.*

Soon he also started to allow limited credit to approved customers.

In 1889 Harrods became a limited liability company, and at the age of fifty Charles Harrod retired. However, he later returned and took charge until the appointment of Richard Burbridge as general manager in 1891. Burbridge was a forceful leader and it was

brushmaker, dentist, shoe-maker, bookseller, gold-smith and fruiterer.

As he prospered he realized he needed more space and opened a new branch, also in Oxford Street, but this proved unsuccessful and soon closed. A little later, how-ever, the corner shop

he who took the store forward towards the splendid building and total site we know today – but that would be in the Edwardian era.

John Lewis was born sixteen months before Queen Victoria came to the throne. In 1864 'Mr John Lewis of Oxford Street', as he liked to be called, resigned his post as buyer of silks and woollen dress materials for Mr Peter Robinson, and started in business with financial help from his sisters in a small single shop, formerly a tobacconist's, which he leased at 132 Oxford Street. He had already worked in drapers' shops in Bridgwater and Liverpool. At that time you could rent a shop, even in Oxford Street, for as little as £1 a week and wholesale houses would give up to six months' credit. Many of the shops were single with living accommoda-tion – Marshall & Snelgrove had six and Peter Robinson four such houses. John Lewis's sign went up among those for a

adjacent to Holles Street became vacant; John Lewis gave a friend a blank cheque and asked him to buy the shop, no matter what the price. He himself went out for an anxious walk, returning to find that he had acquired an extension to his shop at a surprisingly low price. Over the years he gradually expanded

safe life was in those early days, when it was possible for an elderly man to walk each day down to Oxford Circus, carrying a large black bag which obviously had the day's takings in it, take a bus to Trafalgar Square and then walk down the Strand to Coutts Bank without fear of attack! This was during the age when horse-drawn two-wheeled carts were used to deliver goods and all the women employees wore sober black silk dresses in the showrooms. In the shop, on the ground floor, each department had a shop-walker who would sign all the bills, and who, in the absence of the buyer was in charge of the department. When buyers were not away buying they were expected to be in their department – John Lewis had a ruling: 'When

into adjoining properties and widened his range of stock.

John Lewis had been a buyer of dress materials but now he dealt in ribbons and haberdashery (at that time called fancy goods, and very widely used in the age of crinolines), often buying clearance lines at very low prices. He believed in giving the best value but also stocked a wide range of colours and widths of ribbons, cultivating the idea that his was the likeliest shop to stock some unusual colour or style; he also believed every offer should be genuinely attractive, with no hidden snags.

John Lewis's son, Oswald, and younger brother of John Spedan Lewis, recalled many years later how

a man ceases to sell he should cease to buy.'

John Lewis held control of the business for the next forty-two years, retaining absolute power and giving employees as little information as possible; only in 1906 did he take his son, John Spedan Lewis, into business and Oswald in 1908. He continued to work until his death in 1928, when he was ninety-two. He regarded his wife's piano playing as a waste of time and her Christian belief as childish;

John Lewis's own belief, declared his elder son, was in the divine right of employers! In business he was a remarkable man willing to pay enough to secure the services of a particular man for a specific post, but also underpaying other staff to the extent that they often left to work for a competitor. When this happened, he salved his conscience by declaring that it was time for them to leave anyway. By the turn of the century the company had a staff of three hundred.

John Lewis was a Liberal and republican, opposed to trade unions. When he was eighty-four his employees demanded union recognition, but he said this 'would not suit his arrangements' and he won the day, a Victorian employer to the end. It was only after his father's death that his son put into effect the ideas of partnership for which the firm became well known in the twentieth century. John Spedan Lewis experimented with his ideas of partnership at Peter Jones in 1914. The first profit sharing scheme was approved by the Peter Jones shareholders in 1920 and the first Trust Settlement which formally created the John Lewis Partnership was signed in 1929.

Meanwhile, up in Scotland, along Edinburgh's famous Princes Street, developments were also taking place. In 1838 it was already a busy place, with the fishwife, the china-mender, the apple-woman, the coalman and a dozen other hawkers all shouting their wares at the tops of their voices, and over the next 100 years the Street would be widened twice. Down it came the 9 o'clock coach for Glasgow, leaving The Crown Hotel, 1 Princes Street, each morning. It was another four years before Queen Victoria and the Prince Consort

FACING PAGE ABOVE: *This languid lady is from the Liberty Catalogue of 1883.* RIGHT: *The new fashionable provincial towns also boasted prestigious department stores, such as Kendal, Milne & Faulkner of Manchester.* BELOW: *Kennington and Jenner's famous store in Edinburgh.*

visited the city, and by then the railway had arrived. For getting around within the city, those who could afford it used either a sedan chair, carried by two Highlanders, a 'Growler', a four-wheeled horse-drawn carriage, or a 'Minibus', a two-wheeled, square-shaped horse-drawn vehicle into which luggage went first before the passengers sat on the side seats – to stop it on a hill the driver reversed the wheels against the kerb! Into this setting came Charles Kennington and Charles Jenner, finding work with an Edinburgh draper.

They asked their employer for a holiday to go to the Musselburgh Autumn Race Meeting and being refused, went all the same. On their return they were sacked but on 28 April 1838

they advertised in the *Scotsman* that they would open their new premises on Tuesday 1 May. The premises were leased from a tobacco manufacturer and consisted of 'two shops with plate-glass windows, sufficient drains, a new upper floor, sliding window shutters, sun blinds for the windows towards Princes Street, the ceiling finished with a handsome plaster cornice, and with gas pipes into the shop at convenient places'. One shop had previously been used by a music seller, the other by a toy dealer. By 1860 the premises had been extended to take in all of 48 Princes Street (previously divided into three shops) and also 2, 4, 6, and 8 South St David Street. After Charles Kennington's death in 1863 the name became Charles Jenner & Co. Gradually other properties were bought, but in November 1892 a disastrous fire destroyed the premises. However, the new Jenners was officially re-opened in May 1895, built to a design inspired by the Oxford Bodleian Library, although it had actually opened for a Christmas Bazaar in December 1894. The new building was outstanding, with electric light on a lavish scale, air conditioning and fast lifts. A new shopping culture for a new century was about to begin.

New Provincial Fashionable Towns

Shortly before the beginning of Queen Victoria's reign some of our now famous 'quality' towns, such as Cheltenham, Bath and Harrogate started to develop as fashionable provincial centres. In the early 1800s Jane Austen, in her book *Northanger Abbey*, has Miss Morland comment to Mr Tilney, 'Bath is a charming place, sir, there are so many good shops here.' However, it was William Debenham who made the pioneering venture in 1818 when he opened Cavendish House on Cheltenham's Promenade; soon he was attracting the aristocrats, the landed gentry and the new rich industrialists to stay in the town and purchase goods previously only available in London.

When he opened a shop in Harrogate, Debenham's partner, Clement Freebody, found the local traders provided fierce competition.

Later, another famous store, Marshall & Snelgrove, also provided opposition. Harrogate described itself, in a guide book, as one of the 'Queens of English Watering Places'. Although 'Harrogate has no sands, no harbour, and but one 'Ship' – that a small inn – yet in its 'Stray', or common, it possesses a sea of verdant grass over two hundred acres in extent . . . in the heart of the town.' The book also claims that 'when the visitor emerges from the railway station he can hardly fail to remark the exhilarating atmosphere, the genial air of brightness, reflected by its light cheerful buildings, its dry streets and sandy soil, that refuses to harbour water or depress the eye, and its luxuriant foliage. In all these matters Harrogate is invigorating, and the most sluggish liver and ill-conditioned temper, by bad health disturbed, is not more impervious to Harrogate's bright surroundings, than to its most efficacious "Old Sulphur".'

Harrogate had its 'season' and in its guide for 1900, compiled by the editor of the *Harrogate Herald*, this period is recommended to American visitors; indeed 'to see English life in its most fashionable phases one should visit Harrogate in the height of its season'. Already it was claiming to be a health

James St. Harrogate

resort and its high-class hotels, such as the Prince of Wales, Swan, Majestic, and Prospect, were ready to welcome the visitors, some of whom regarded 'their' hotel as their own house. There were also other private hotels, one claiming that the 'House . . . is exceptionally airy and well ventilated, and warmed with hot water during winter months. Cycle accommodation. The sanitary arrangements are certified.'

Among the 'Amusements' provided for visitors to Harrogate are 'Fashionable Promenades at the Wells, 7.30 to 9am, and in the afternoon [at] Bogs Valley gardens, the Municipal Band'. The Municipal Orchestra gave daily concerts, the Temperance Brass Band also played for the enjoyment of visitors, and of course horse-drawn cabs could be hired, or for those who preferred, bath chairs were available for 1s 3d an hour. At that time there were seventy-five beds at the Bath hospital and a further fifty in the Convalescent Home.

The Harrogate Improvement Commissioner, appointed by the Improvement Act of 1841, had taken the powers to make bye-laws for regulating and carrying on business, for protection of the public wells, for instituting a charge for using the Pump Room, to flag footways at the sides of the streets, to borrow money within certain limits, to light up streets and also cause streets to be cleansed and

SOFT SAWDER.

"BUT I DON'T CALL THIS A FASHIONABLE 'AT!"
"IT WILL SOON *BECOME* SO, MADAM, IF *YOU* WEAR IT!"

rubbish to be removed from the houses. However, householders were required each week, before 10am on a Saturday, to sweep and clean the footways adjacent to their properties, failure to do so resulting in a penalty of five shillings. The benefits of the Act were the careful and planned growth of a modern town, and that included an attractive shopping area.

FACING PAGE: *James Street, 'The Bond Street of Harrogate'.*
RIGHT: *The Spa Esplanade, Scarborough,* The Graphic, *1888.*

As early as 1844, E Little of Canton House was begging to inform 'the visitors of Harrogate', through *The Illustrated London News*, that he had opened a new shop opposite the Royal Cheltenham Pump Room, in Low Harrogate. He pointed out that he had tea, coffee and spices, all of the very best quality, which he had purchased for cash, 'and selling for the same'.

In the 1860s the creation of fashionable James Street began (claimed by some advertisers of the period to be 'The Bond Street of Harrogate') and in 1874 in nearby Cambridge Street a market hall was developed, at a cost of £3,504, which sold meat, fish, fruit, game and other miscellaneous items, with many 'carts from the country bearing all the freshest produce the farm, field, orchard and vinery could produce'. There had been debate in the town about the creation of a market since the early 1840s, but many of the hoteliers were content with the hawkers who brought fresh produce to their establishments, and so the project kept on receiving no action.

As a new century began, the writers of the town guide were able to report 'Harrogate may have been counted dull . . . All that is changed now, and few places can offer more varied attractions, both to the youthful and advanced pleasure seeker . . . Harrogate has nurtured new generations in progressive thought and enterprise . . .'.

Antonio Fattorini, an Italian, established his quality jewellery business in the town in the early years of the reign. He had started his career on market stalls selling pots and pans, knee pads and fancy goods but now he had achieved his ambition. He had seven sons, one of

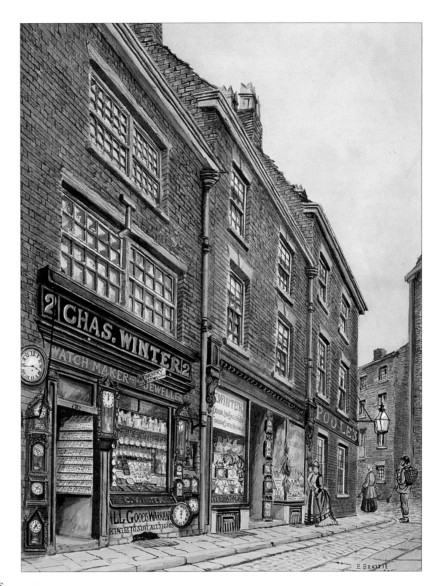

whom, Innocent, became a working jeweller in Skipton, and later members of the family were to be responsible for the founding of Empire Stores and Grattan Warehouse, today two of the best-known names in mail order shopping. Antonio Fattorini opened in Harrogate at the 'Oriental Lounge' in Regent Parade; he advertised to 'the Visitors and Inhabitants of Harrogate' that he had a large stock of jewellery, Sheffield plated goods and Berlin silver which he was offering at exceptionally low prices. He also offered ladies and gentlemen's dressing cases, writing desks, work boxes, umbrellas, parasols, cut glass decanters – a wonderful range of goods for the new upper and middle classes who came to taste the waters of the spa or promenade its streets and green areas. As house building developed in the town several small quarries supplied stone for these ventures and stones of high quality quartz found in these quarries became known as 'Harrogate Diamonds'.

Perhaps this inspired another jeweller, James R Ogden to open his shop in Cambridge Street in 1893, for he called it 'The Little Diamond Shop'. In later years he became an influential man in the town and his workshops created many beautiful items of jewellery and silverware.

For those who 'took the waters' the aroma of toffee being cooked in open pans must have been pleasant relief after the pungent smell of the sulphur waters. No doubt they also queued in the toffee shop to buy this sweetmeat to take

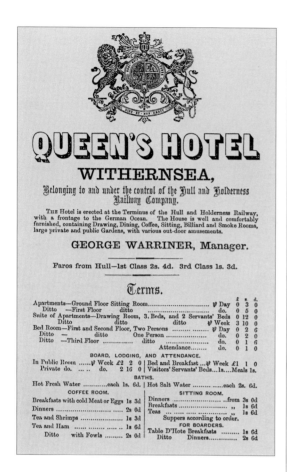

away the taste of the health giving liquid. The detailed story behind Farrah's Harrogate Toffee, now famous throughout the world, is unfortunately lost in the mists of time but it seems that Ann Farrah, who died in 1843 aged seventy-four, was probably its originator. Her son, Joseph Farrah, a 'Shopkeeper and Dealer in Groceries and Sundries' in 1848 had premises at 2 Crescent Place, not far from the Pump Room. It wasn't until 1887 that John Farrah, Joseph's son, registered ''Farrah's Harrogate Toffee' to establish his as the original, for by then others were claiming that they also sold Harrogate Toffee.

It was not only the inland watering towns that became fashionable resorts in Victorian times; Scarborough on the Yorkshire coast also had its 'season', catered for rich visitors and became a very fashionable resort, being highly favoured during the 1850s and 1860s. At that time it had 3 banks, 7 booksellers and stationers, 13 chemists, 45 tailors, 5 bathing machine proprietors and 37 butchers, and a very large number of lodging house keepers. Osbert Sitwell in *Two Generations* describes it as follows:' . . . the season flamed almost exotically through the town in July, August and September, and continued through October and November. In the summer the terraces by the sea were heavy under the sun with patchouli and cigar-smoke, and the streets were full of elegant carriages, drawn by high-stepping, thin-ankled horses, the public houses crowded with footmen at noon. In the evenings, the stone decks of The Spa, designed by Sir Joseph Paxton rustled with the swaying crinolines, and echoed the blare of the German band, while rockets traced their ascending lines into the sky and then blossomed into showers of stars, pink, green and yellow.'

In London, at 11 Vere Street, James Marshall opened a shop in partnership with a Mr Wilson in 1836. James, the youngest of twelve children, had come from Yorkshire to work with Burrell, Son and Toby, a drapery shop at 10 Vere Street. Later John Snelgrove, the son of a Wells paper manufacturer, went to work for Marshall & Wilson, having walked to London with only half-a-crown in his pocket, and in 1848 became a partner in the firm. Perhaps it was because of James Marshall's Yorkshire connections that, at an early date, Marshall & Snelgrove established a shop in Huntriss Row, Scarborough, later moving to Harcourt Place and then St Nicholas Street, near to the town's large hotels, but they only opened for 'the season'.

Nearby, also in St Nicholas Street, was the Old Bank and the York City and County Bank, whilst the London & Yorkshire Bank was located in Westborough. Also in Westborough was the furnishing, upholstering and carpet establishment of Messrs Parker & Cross, not far

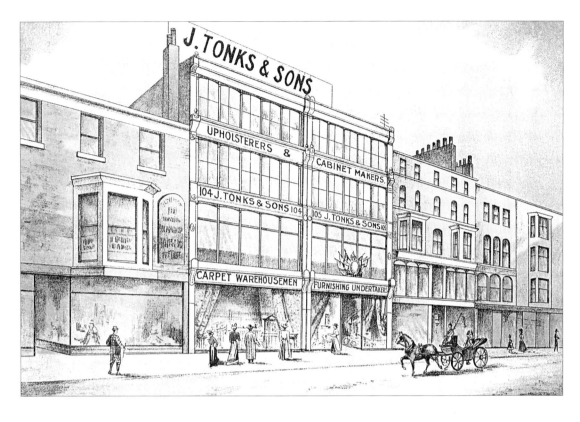

ABOVE: *J. Tonks & Sons, Westborough, Scarborough, 1900.*

away from W Rowntree & Son's magnificent millinery, dress and drapery establishment, which was founded in 1780 by Robert Clemesha. The author of *Peerless Scarborough* claims that these shops were 'in no degree inferior to the best London houses'. The latter firm had a notable reputation in the early part of Victoria's reign as hat makers, but at the end of the century built a carpet room to display imports from China, India, Japan, Persia, and Turkey. It also carried stocks of Royal Doulton and Royal Worcester porcelain and proudly proclaimed that it possessed an "hydraulic lift from basement to roof", electric light in all parts, and that a cosy tea-room and new counting-house accommodation were also being added. The company also held agencies for Liberty's, Dr Jaeger's sanitary woollen garments, and Butterick's paper patterns, which 'enable a lady to renew her wardrobe at a comparatively nominal cost'. *Scarborough – Ancient & Modern* tells us that 'creature comforts are secured through the agency of a high class restaurant on the promenade, presided over by Mr. Councillor Topham, and Messrs Rowntree have cosy tents and tea rooms wherein the fair sex indulge in "five o'clock tea" and the latest gossip, while the gentlemen run up big scores – on the billiard table'. It is from this branch of the Rowntree family that the York chocolatiers come.

At the close of the nineteenth century Scarborough had 11 hotels that offered billiard rooms, 5 banks, 6 bath chair proprietors, 3 donkey proprietors 20 hosiers and glovers, 6 mineral and aerated water manufacturers, 19 booksellers and stationers, 22 chemists, 9 cocoa houses, 10 game and poultry dealers, 20 laundries, and 49 tailors.

Pedlars, Fairs and Markets

In earlier centuries, it would not be unusual to see cattle, animals and produce being sold on the streets every day. However, by the time Queen Victoria had come to the throne, many Highway Acts had been passed and towns were starting to develop into recognizable centres of commerce and business. By 1850 this development had become quite pronounced and properties in the principal streets were able to command high rents.

Today it is difficult for us to visualize the street scenes of the Victorian years, life has changed so much. Fortunately, early photographs and newspaper and magazine articles give us an insight into daily life, and also those special 'high days' of Victorian England. In the 1880s Charles Spurgeon – a twin son of Rev Charles Haddon Spurgeon, who was at that time the renowned minister of London's Metropolitan Tabernacle – took a series of photographs in Greenwich, showing the common life of the day and contemporary paintings and prints give a glimpse of the diversity of street life.

Although fairs had been important in pre-Victorian times, few were now held in the streets. When they were held, it was generally as occasions to sell agricultural produce at the end of a season or to hire labour, but by this period they had generally become more social events for the working classes, and

FACING PAGE: *Whilst fashionable stores attracted an increasing number of quality shoppers, the poor remained dependent on street markets for most goods as shown in this painting of* Lambeth Market *by Godefroy Durand (1873–77).*
RIGHT: *Household goods as well as food were sold in street markets and from barrows.*

were often associated with drinking and rowdiness.

Markets were generally regarded, in the early years of the period, as relating to gatherings of itinerant retailers in the open air, on pre-determined days each week, in a country town. Then, as now, those doing the selling were often the people who had grown the produce, or made the items

they were selling; the buyers were often looking for a bargain, expecting that as the seller had less overheads the prices would be lower. In the 1850s, when many towns were still surrounded by market gardens and fields where animals could be grazed, local people and also many who travelled in from the surrounding countryside, would attend the market to buy and sell fresh produce.

Other items sold at such markets would be cheaper clothes, including second-hand ones, and lower grades of footwear, particularly boots and shoes suitable for those working on the land. An account of a London street market operated in 1851, describes how a market trader toured the streets offering flowers – fuchsias, geraniums and mignonettes – in return for any old clothes he could persuade local residents to part with. The buyer didn't really value old trousers, much preferring an old skirt which could be used to make cloth caps for boys. After much haggling the deal was done and the man would move on down the road hoping to make another transaction. Gradually the man's long black bag would be filled and then he would make his way down to the Old Clothes Mart.

There one was met by the stench of the accumulated old clothes and rags – a mustiness, mouldiness, and fustiness, a peculiar sour smell. Many of the sellers were eager Jews, some with long grizzly beards, and others in greasy gabardines; there was a great bustle, an eagerness among the buyers of London's refuse. Here were long wooden benches, partly covered by eaves-like roofing; here were to be found bottle swoppers, juvenile purloiners of lead, barterers of crockery-ware for old clothes, the flower swoppers, umbrella menders, and the motley collection of petty dealers and chapmen, all with their goods in a heap in front of them. Almost all would seem worthless and yet to its seller it represented his stock in trade.

The buyers themselves were just as motley a group as the sellers. They represented several nationalities; some had come

FACING PAGE: *Costermongers prepare their goods for market at* Covent Garden Market, *c 1870 by John Thompson.*
ABOVE: *This picture from* The Illustrated London News *shows the opening of the great cheese market hall at Chippenham in 1850.*
LEFT: Punch *magazine was ready as ever to point out the rivalry that accompanied the new shopping boom, even amongst costermongers.*

TRUE RESPECTABILITY.

First Costermonger. "I WONDER A RESPECTABLE COVE LIKE YOU, BILL, CARRIES YOUR OWN COLLYFLOWERS; WHY DON'T YER KEEP A CARRIDGE LIKE MINE?"

Second Costermonger. "WHY DON'T I KEEP A CARRIDGE? WHY, BECAUSE I DON'T CHOOSE TO WASTE MY HINCUM IN MERE SHOW AND FASHIONABLE DISPLAY!"

was sold by journey-men who made up cheap items for the working classes.

John Upson was one of those who started selling shoes from a barrow in London's Woolwich Market; this was in 1863. Often he would work late into the night, particularly on a Saturday, and eventually he graduated from the barrow to a large stall. Later he opened his first shop, in Woolwich, trading as 'Upson The Great Boot Provider'. More and more shops followed in south-east London under this name, under the Upson name and the names of C W Barron & Company, and High Life Shoe Company; these latter ones

to buy old rough charity clothing or army great-coats for the Irish market, some women were buying up the left-off wardrobes of the nobility to sell to the actresses of the minor theatres. Among all this are those who offer their own refreshment – hot peas, hot eels or mutton hooves. Often the traders worked in pairs, especially where one of them could not read.

Although richer households would use china and earthenware, most poorer families used pots, and those selling pottery would travel from market to market. Similarly, furniture

LEFT: *Petticoat Lane market (1889),
like all street markets of the time,
was thought to attract thieves and
pickpockets.*
FACING PAGE, ABOVE: *A further example
of the spirit of healthy competition
amongst the street traders of Victorian England as seen in* Punch.
BELOW: *Pedlars and street traders
often specialized in ribbons and
lace as shown in this painting,*
The Outdoor Haberdashery, *by
Augustus Jules Bouvier(1837–81).*

on behalf of the upper-class households where they worked.

In urban towns indoor markets were developed and many of these buildings still exist. Often specific sections, or even whole buildings, were given over to a particular area, such as fish, meat, fruit and vegetables, clothing, hardware, etc.

The hawker and pedlar, whilst not synonymous, were very similar, and also there were the barrow-boys. Often the street trader would cry his wares and in *The Graphic* of 1888

being existing companies he purchased. Soon he, and his son Frederick, had nearly a hundred shops. By the time of the First World War the company had fourteen shops in Oxford Street alone. It was shortly after this time that the company started using the name Dolcis for its shops.

While most of those attending the markets would be working-class people, in some cases domestic servants would purchase provisions

there were reports that the residents of Brixton were complaining about this, although it was made clear that this was not the only locality where there was a problem. Such disturbances were worst in poor neighbourhoods and were particularly upsetting for invalids and nervous old folks – what could be more distracting to them than the sudden appearance of half-a-dozen strong-lunged fellows with barrows, all

shouting "Mackerel, six a shilling" at the top
of their voices? The article suggested that the
English had become more musical than they
were, 'but in the matter of street cries there had
been a distinct regression'! Tongue in cheek,
the journalist suggests: 'Why should not artistic
street-crying be taught in Board School?'

In the 1880s it was frequently Italians who
vended ice creams (they often sold roast chest-
nuts in winter) in the streets. There was concern at the danger to children's health, caused
by the preparation of the ice creams in filthy
conditions, and from impure materials such
as sour milk and acid flavourings. Additionally,
they were often served in lead-pots which led
to a risk of lead poisoning. An item about this
in *The Graphic* was the result of an inquest on

"BETWEEN TWO SHOEBLACKS WE FALL," &c.

First Shoeblack. "I COTCHED 'OLD ON HIM FUST!"
Second Ditto. "YOU'RE A——"　　　[*Old Gentleman is flung heavily.*]

MUCH TOO CLEVER.

Sharp (but vulgar) Little Boy. "HALLO, MISSUS, WOT ARE THOSE?"
Old Woman. "TWOPENCE."
Boy. "WHAT A LIE! THEY'RE APPLES."

[Exit, whistling popular air.

a little girl, where the inquest jury called for samples of ice creams sold in the streets to be analysed to protect poor children.

Soon after Michael Marks arrived in Leeds in 1884 he began peddling goods in the villages around the city. He had met Isaac Dewhirst, and Charlie Backhouse, Isaac's general manager, outside the wholesale warehouse in Kirkgate where Dewhirst sold goods to market traders and the tenants of cheap shops. Dewhirst loaned Michael Marks £5, a considerable sum in those days, and Michael bought goods to that value from him.

Michael Marks was not a healthy person and as soon as he could afford to do so he hired a pitch on Leeds open-air market, where his stall was a 6ft by 3ft trestle table. He developed good relationships with the staff at Dewhirst's and daily went to the warehouse to replenish his stock. It was there he met Tom

Spencer who was the cashier. Having gained a knowledge of people's needs and wants while working as a pedlar, he did very well. Now he spent two days a week at his stall in Leeds, and took stalls at markets in Castleford and Wakefield on the other days. Before long Dewhirst's were supplying him with girls to work on the stalls so he could go to other markets, thereby having two stalls on the same day.

Gradually Michael Marks's enterprise grew. He moved to a permanent stall in Leeds' new covered Market Hall, and above it put a poster stating 'M Marks: the original Penny Bazaar'. Within two years he had stalls in covered market halls in towns throughout Yorkshire and Lancashire, and was even represented as far away as Cardiff. The next development was to have a chain of stores throughout England and Wales. The fronts of the shops were open during trading hours and there were counters down both sides and across the back.

In 1894 he opened a large shop in Manchester, and started trading directly with manufacturers. Perhaps most importantly, certainly from an historical viewpoint, he formed a partnership with Tom Spencer – Marks & Spencer had been born!

Barrow boys were very much part of London life in this era and would sell anything from crockery to fish or fruit. In London, barrows could be hired in the 1850s at 3d a day or 1s a week in the six winter months, or from 4d a day or 1s 6d a week in the summer. In Greenwich, crockery would be sold not only to housewives, but also to hotel and restaurant keepers, for there were many restaurants there at that time. In coastal areas, fish was common, but in the early years before transport systems had developed, was less so in the heart of the country. Very popular was White Bait, not a particular species of fish, but rather a mixture of young fish, predominantly herrings and sprats. In those days, when many London suburbs were still near to, or in the countryside, rabbits were commonplace, and hawkers would transport them on a short pole carried over the shoulder – a rabbit would make a good meal for a family. He would also, no doubt, call out his wares in the street and would have regular 'big houses' where he would go to the back door to sell them to the cook.

In streets where each passing horse-drawn vehicle posed a health risk from dust, or worse, it would have been difficult to keep merchandise clean. Sometimes it was not always as 'clean' as it might be in another sense, for as early as 1889 *Chambers's Journal* suggested that some people, knowing the 'gullibility' of an Englishman's character, would set up an 'establishment', draw a large crowd and then 'attract

STATE O' TRADE.

Small Girl. "PLEASE, MRS. GREENSTOUGH, MOTHER SAYS WILL YOU GIVE HER A LETTUCE ?"
Mrs. G. "GIVE ?! TELL THEE MOTHER GIV'UM'S DEAD, AND LENDUM'S VERY BAD. NOTHINK FOR NOTHINK 'ERE, AND PRECIOUS LITTLE FOR SIXPENCE !!"

A CHANGE FOR THE BETTER.

Greengrocer. "WANT A PENN'ORTH O' COALS, DO YER ? YOU WON'T BE ABLE TO 'AVE A PENN'ORTH MUCH LONGER. THEY'RE A GOING UP. COALS IS COALS NOW, I CAN TELL YER !"
Boy. "AH, WELL, MOTHER'LL BE GLAD O' THAT, 'CAUSE SHE SAYS THE LAST COALS SHE HAD O' YOU WAS ALL *SLATES* !!"

into his own pockets some of the superfluous metal which reposes in those of his hearers'. Sometimes the goods are 'quack remedies', such as flagroot – the root of an iris, stained to a brownish tint, perfumed with a few drops of bergamot, and passed off as an Indian herb, to be grated and taken like snuff to relieve headaches, or rubbed on the gums to relieve toothache. The seller assures the crowd that he is a philanthropist, only concerned for the goodness of their health! Another trader uses an open carriage as a base and sells other 'proprietary remedies', whilst others sell 'wedding rings' at a penny each, or corn cures — the market place and surrounding streets was full of such people. These 'street traders' will dispose of worthless goods in a matter of hours and then adjourn to the local tavern. Sadly some things never change!

The Co-operative Store

The Rochdale Pioneers opened their shop in Toad Lane, Rochdale in December 1844. Whilst it was not the first co-operative endeavour it was the one from which the movement marks its starting point.

The Rochdale Equitable Pioneers Society developed their 'Principles of Co-operation', and these were taken up by other such societies as they were formed; they are:

The present Co-operative Movement does not intend to meddle with the various religious or political differences which are now existing in society, but by a common bond, namely that of self interest, to join together the means, the energies, and the talents of all for the common benefit of each.

1. That capital should be of their own providing and bear a fixed rate of interest.

2. That only the purest provisions procurable should be supplied to members.

3. That full weight and measure should be given.

4. That market prices should be charged and no credit given nor asked.

5. That profits should be divided pro rata upon the amount of purchases made by each member.

6. That the principle of 'one member one vote' should obtain in government and the equality of the sexes in membership.

7. That the management should be in the hands of officers and committee elected periodically.

8. That a definite percentage of profits should be allotted to education.

9. That frequent statements and balance sheets should be presented to members.

They also spelt out the objects of the Society which were to improve the social and domestic condition of the members by: raising capital in

shares of £1 each, to enable them to establish a store for the sale of provisions, clothing etc; building or purchasing a number of houses to be occupied by members; manufacturing articles, thus providing employment for members who were without work or who were suffering from repeated reductions in their wages; and by purchasing an estate, or estates of land, which would be cultivated by those members who were out of work or badly paid. The objects went further by stating that as soon as practicable the Society 'shall proceed to arrange the powers of production, distribution, education and government, or in other words, to establish a self-supporting home colony of united interests, or assist other societies in establishing such colonies'. It was also proposed 'that for the promotion of sobriety, a temperance hotel be opened in one of the Society's houses as soon as convenient'.

floor for £10 a year, converting the front room into a shop. Above them were rooms used as a chapel.

The Pioneers had only £28 to launch their business – for them no elaborate shop furniture, just a simple bench for customers, a desk for the cashier and white-washed walls at 31 Toad Lane, Rochdale. This building had been erected in 1790 as a warehouse, and they rented the ground

The interiors shown here are authentic reproductions of Victorian Co-operative stores which stocked every kind of provision and household requirement.

Initially, the shop was open on only two evenings a week, from about 8 o'clock until 10, selling sugar, butter, flour, oatmeal and tallow candles. Gradually however, the range was increased and included tea and tobacco. The back room was used to store the goods and was also where the directors would meet to conduct their business.

The rules of the Society determined that it was a democratic body with a president, treasurer and secretary, three trustees and five directors, each to be elected annually by general meetings of members. These officers were responsible to the membership and at quarterly meetings gave account of their governance and considered the audited financial reports. The officers and directors met weekly and the duties and responsibilities of each officer were clearly defined; any disputes were settled by arbitrators, none of whom could be those directly or indirectly interested in the funds of the Society.

As the Society prospered the Pioneers also rented the upper floors of the building, the first floor becoming a library and class-room whilst the upper floor housed a small drapery and shoe-repairing section.

In 1850 a co-operative corn mill was started by some men in Rochdale and the Pioneers invested £100 in the venture; the law did not allow such Societies to have shares in similar societies, and therefore the Pioneers had to appoint representatives to hold the shares. This was the start of further implementing their original objectives. A later venture associated with the Rochdale Pioneers was the formation of the Rochdale Provident Sick and Burial Society. The Society was also instrumental in the establishment of the Co-operative Wholesale Society.

Around the country other similar societies had come into existence independently, following the Rochdale example, some serving rural villages whilst others met the needs of those who lived in or around the larger cities.

For a better understanding of the reason for the formation of societies, we need to examine the social conditions in the early part of Queen Victoria's reign. Many local Yorkshire people, for example, worked on

The Co-operative Brotherhood Trust Ltd, Newington Green Road, London, started in 1897 and became part of the London Co-operative Society in 1921.

JARROW AND HEBBURN CO-OPERATIVE STORES, HILL STREET BRANCH.

small farms or were employed by one of the textile mill owners, either in the mill or as 'outworkers', hand-loom weavers working in their isolated cottages, earning very little and much of that being paid in goods from the mill-owner's shop. The dwellings of such people were rented and generally consisted of one storey and only one room, furnished with 'a pair of looms, a bobbin wheel, a half-headed turn-up bedstead (the bed itself being made of chaff), a round table standing on three legs, a few turned unpainted chairs, an old chest and a cradle'. Very few had a clock, a chest of drawers or a second bedstead, the adults and children all having to sleep together. The food was also basic, consisting of oatmeal porridge with milk for breakfast, and potatoes with a bit of bacon fried together, with a piece of oat-cake dipped in the fat, for dinner. An ounce of tea had to last a week, or if it ran out, mint or herbs became a substitute; butter was only available on Sundays and flour and wheat bread were regarded as luxuries.

It was against such conditions that discontent grew and the men continually discussed ways of improving their lot, not least through support for the Chartist movement and also the formation of co-operative ventures.

A 'co-op' had been started in 1842 but had not lasted. In June 1859 the Great Horton Industrial Self-Help Society was formed and over the next few weeks subscriptions were received to form its first capital; by 16 July the members had £13 4s. Now they made their first purchase, two sacks of flour which cost them £2 14s 6d; the following week they recorded: 'Flour sould [sic], £1 12s 9d'. Gradually the amounts purchased and sold both grew and the range of items was also expanded. At first they only opened on a Friday evening, part of a house serving as a shop. These first officers and members had no previous practical experience but were prepared to risk their savings and be stewards of the capital contributed by their fellow townsmen; they were men of integrity, of strong conviction, who were prepared to work hard to attain success.

Soon they were able to rent a shop, 75 High Street, and open for longer hours, such was the public's confidence in them; Samuel Watmough was appointed their first 'shopman' and remained so until 1871. Within two years of the formation of the Society a branch shop was opened at Wibsey, about a mile away, and a further shop was opened at Low Moor in the same year. On 2 October 1861 – when they had only 700 members and capital of £3,084 – they passed a resolution to build central premises for the Society. The venture was to cost them £3,760, exclusive of fixtures, and therefore a mortgage of £1,800 was arranged. In July 1863, amid great jubilation, the new premises were opened. They were four storeys high, including basement, and consisted of a grocer's, draper's and butcher's shops, with plate-glass windows, on the ground floor, whilst on the first floor were storerooms and showrooms for the grocer's and draper's departments, and milliners' and tailors' work rooms; on the top floor was a music hall which would seat 700 people. This hall became the centre of attraction for many community events. In 1863 the Society had 614 members, capital of £3,084 and sales of £8,087; by 1869 these figures had risen to 851 members, £6,583 capital and sales of £23,798 – in those few years sales had risen 194 per cent! In 1870 'improved' working hours came, the shop now closing at 8pm on Mondays, 1pm on Tuesdays, 8.30pm on Wednesdays, 9pm on Thursdays and Saturdays and 10pm on Fridays!

A few miles away in the rural landscape of Hepworth, not far from Huddersfield, a Society had been formed in 1840. Its first premises were a cottage shop to which one of its farming members brought butter and another supplied potatoes. Later another member, John Holmes, killed his pig and, after the carcass

had been cured, he brought bacon and ham to add to the co-operative provisions. Steadily the custom grew and the directors purchased direct from local farmers and growers. It was the men of the community who were generally the members of the Society (Esther Kaye was the only woman member in 1843) but its success depended on the shopping loyalty of their wives, who had been accustomed to doing their shopping in the nearby market towns.

The Co-operative Wholesale Society was formed in 1863 and in 1869 built its well-known premises in Balloon Street, Manchester; the Co-operative Bank was also located there. The building served not just as offices but also contained showrooms for practically everything, from Furnishing to Stationery. Individual members of small village Societies, living near to the city, were able to go and inspect the stocks – carpets, furniture or jewellery for example – thereby having the same advantages as a member of a larger Society. Also, a manager from a smaller society could select the goods for his shop or department from ranges at the CWS and these would then be distributed to his store in hampers, ready to be displayed.

In adjacent CWS buildings warehousing was provided for the Grocery Department, the Boot and Shoe Department, and Drapery, while all over the country were factories and warehouses able to supply almost all the needs of the individual societies.

Working at 'The Co-op' was seen as a good job, not least because many Societies offered training in the Co-operative Hall. Here in an evening staff would learn the art of being a salesperson and also the skill of bookkeeping. The working day would generally start at 8 o'clock, but they would be expected to be at their places, ready for customers before the hour struck. Each member had a check number (I remember my grandmother's was 101 AE) and this was entered on the check, in triplicate, when a purchase was made. The customer kept the top copy, the next went to the cash office and the third one was kept in the department as a record of the day's sales. Once a quarter 'the divi' was calculated and could then be used for further purchases, but many people kept it as a reserve against hard times or when extra items were needed.

Co-operative stores were generally accepted by the public, but they had their opponents in the trade. It was however agreed that the cash settlements which they insisted upon had been good for all traders.

The developments at Rochdale, and those that followed in other parts of the country, were the initiatives of working-class people. However, in 1864 a group of clerks at the London General Post Office bought a chest of tea and discovered that they could save 9d on each pound; soon they bought other groceries, with similar savings, and in 1866 created the Civil Service Supply Association. In 1868 they opened a shop in the Strand and gradually the Association was able to supply other household goods, clothing and many other items, all from the one shop.

When co-operative trading by civil servants commenced, as in the Army & Navy Stores, or as it was known at that time, the Army & Navy Co-operative Society, there was a certain amount of concern and this was expressed in an item in *The Illustrated London News* in 1879: 'On behalf of the shopkeepers it is urged that civil servants ought not to be allowed to meddle with retail trading.' However private shopkeepers are told that 'if only they will do business on the same terms they, being skilled in their respective callings, ought to be able to beat mere amateurs.' Such was the feeling expressed by tradesmen and governing bodies that they called a meeting at the Westminster District Board of Works to protest.

When first established, the Army & Navy Co-operative Society was only 'open' to its own members. In 1871 a small group of officers who were concerned at the high price of wine started to order it by the case, and thereby only pay wholesale prices. The initial idea was to

RETAIL TRADERS v. CO-OPERATIVE STORES.
JOHN THOMAS IS EMPHATICALLY ON THE SIDE OF THE FORMER.

supply members with high quality goods at the lowest price. To avoid having to have a large capital sum members were required either to pay in to deposit accounts or to pay cash.

Its first premises were in Victoria Street, London, at that time a new road which had been driven through the slums between Westminster Abbey and Victoria Station. Only officers and non-commissioned officers, their families and others introduced by them, but vetted by the Board, were able to be members; the membership subscription was 5s for the first year and subsequently 2s 6d a year. The premises had no display windows, but inside had reading rooms, writing rooms and cloak-rooms, and from 9.15 to 11am breakfast was served in the refreshment room.

For members serving or living overseas an annual catalogue kept them in touch and enabled them to make their purchases.

It has been said that the Army & Navy Stores supplied a member's needs from the cradle to the grave – indeed it did supply the cradle and layette, and also provided a funeral service and erected his memorial! In the in-between years it provided his baby clothes, his sports equipment when he was at school, later his guns, fishing rods and golf clubs, later still his visiting cards and wedding needs. It found him a house or flat, supplied his coals, would even wind his clocks (if he was within a certain distance of London), offered him a laundry service, provided theatre tickets, and also developed a lending library. If he was going abroad the 'Stores', as it was affec-tionately known to its members, offered a stor-age service for his goods, whilst also providing a ticket reservation service, and an opportunity to buy a carrying chair, in order that he might be borne through the tropical jungle by natives.

As early as 1874 the Society started to manufacture goods at Victoria Street but factories were later acquired elsewhere in London. Probably best known was the watch factory where, even in late Victorian times, it made clocks which had three dials, showing the time at Greenwich, Calcutta and Bombay.